Morgan Dix

Historical Recollections of St. Paul's Chapel, New York

Morgan Dix

Historical Recollections of St. Paul's Chapel, New York

ISBN/EAN: 9783744641104

Printed in Europe, USA, Canada, Australia, Japan

Cover: Foto ©ninafisch / pixelio.de

More available books at **www.hansebooks.com**

HISTORICAL RECOLLECTIONS

OF

S. PAUL'S CHAPEL, NEW YORK.

BY THE

REV. MORGAN DIX, S. T. D.,

RECTOR OF TRINITY CHURCH.

TO WHICH IS PREFIXED

AN ACCOUNT OF THE THREE DAYS' SERVICES HELD IN THAT
CHAPEL ON OCCASION OF THE CELEBRATION OF ITS
CENTENNIAL ANNIVERSARY,

Oct. 28th, 29th, and 30th, 1866.

PRINTED BY ORDER OF THE VESTRY OF TRINITY CHURCH.

NEW YORK:
F. J. HUNTINGTON AND COMPANY,
459 BROOME STREET.
1867.

INTRODUCTORY NARRATIVE.

IT was on the 30th day of October, in the year of our Lord 1766, that the Chapel of Saint Paul, in the parish of Trinity Church, in the City of New York, was first opened for the worship of Almighty GOD. Upon the approach of the hundredth anniversary of that day, the subject was formally brought before the Vestry of Trinity Church by the Rector of the parish; and at his request a special committee was appointed to act with him in making arrangements for the due observance of the occasion. This committee consisted of five, as follows: Messrs. Wm. E. Dunscomb, Henry Youngs, Samuel Davis, Benjamin R. Winthrop, and John Travers. Frequent meetings were held, before and after the Centennial, as circumstances required; and the Rector avails himself of this opportunity to offer to those gentlemen his thanks for their services, and for their cordial co-operation in the plans and suggestions which were, from time to time, presented by him for their consideration.

It was decided, after due reflection, to observe the Centennial by a series of services, to continue during three days; and, since the 30th of October fell on a Tuesday, it was further decided to commence the commemoration on the preceding Sunday. It was also thought best that, on each of the three days, there should be a solemn celebration of the

Holy Eucharist, since that has always been regarded as the highest act of Christian worship, the distinctive expression of praise and thanksgiving, and the spiritual sacrifice of the children of God. Several of the Clergy of the parish were invited to prepare discourses on topics in harmony with the occasion ; and, in view of the antiquity of the building, and the many events of historical importance which have transpired within or near it, the Rector undertook to prepare a narrative-lecture, in which there should be recorded such facts and well-authenticated traditions concerning S. Paul's as deserve to be held in remembrance. Moreover, since the attention of our own branch of the Church is now drawn to the subject of the Choral Service, and since a growing love of that ancient and delightful mode of worship is happily perceptible among us, it was thought advisable that, of the many services of the three days, some should be performed with the aid of a competent choir of men and boys, in hope of presenting, at that memorable time, a more than ordinarily impressive tribute of gratitude for past mercies, through the instrumentality of the Choral Song. Such were the general outlines of the plan. The statement of details will be made in the order of the successive days of this observance.

SUNDAY, OCTOBER 28TH.

Feast of S. Simon and S. Jude, and 22d Sunday after Trinity.

The beauty of the American autumnal days, so widely lauded and so intensely enjoyed, could not have had a more favorable illustration than on this first day of the week. A large congregation assembled at the usual hour of morning service in the venerable building. And here it seems proper to mention the decorations which had been made, as free-will offerings, by some devout persons who valued the privilege of giving in this way to the house of the LORD and the shrine of His Presence. These decorations, though few and simple, were rich and costly ; and confined almost exclusively to the chancel and altar. The reading-desk and pulpit were furnished with frontals of white merino, beautifully embroidered in silk by a lady of the congregation, and similar hangings covered the book-boards of the sedilia within the sacrarium. In and about the chancel stood cedars and arbor-vitæ trees, of great size and beauty; these had been brought from the country-seat of a family of the congregation, and were selected with great care for that sacred office of making beautiful the place of the sanctuary. The altar was vested in an entirely new and lovely garb; the frontal and super-frontal were of the richest white moiré, exceeding costly; the frontal being relieved by vertical orphreys or bands of red and gold silk, embroidered with the sacred monogram, and enriched with gold-colored silk fringe. These vestings of the Holy Table were not returned around the ends; but the "fair, white linen cloth," perfectly plain, without embroidery, covered the top of the altar, and fell over either end to the foot-pace. The altar-ledge bore, as usual, the cross and vases: it was one bed of living flowers, which were connected by long trailing branches of ivy, with more flowers in the ledges and window-sills above; while pots of flowers and flowering shrubs were set on the footpace at the north and south ends of the Lord's Table. The vestments of the altar were the gift of one member of the congregation, who, rich in faith and good deeds, and hitherto an efficient helper of the Clergy in their work among the poor, made this noble offering to the Lord from the savings of her laborious trade, patiently laid by for a long time past, with a view to this final disposition. The font was filled with choice and fragrant flowers; and in the chancel, at either end of the altar, stood candelabra with wax candles. The flowers were renewed, from time to time, during the continuance of the festival.

The hour of Divine Service, 10½ o'clock A. M., having arrived, the officiating Clergy, the Rev. Rector, the Rev. Benj. I. Haight, D. D., and the Rev. Frederick B. Van Kleeck, A. M., entered the church, and proceeded with the Morning Prayer, Litany, and Ante-Communion Service, as usual. Instead of the Psalter for the day, Proper Psalms were chanted, being the 16th, the 19th, and the 53d. The Nicene Creed was sung to the 8th Gregorian tone. After the Gospel, an Anthem by Stevenson was sung; the words being taken from Ps. viii., " O Lord, our Governor."

The sermon at this opening service was preached by the Rev. Dr. Haight. His text was Ps. cv. 1–6. In this discourse, which appropriately introduced the series, after due commemoration of the mercies of the past century, the preacher gave many interesting recollections of persons who have in former years worshipped in S. Paul's, referring to clergymen, vestrymen, and others, now departed from us. The discourse was of the nature of a brief memorial of the faithful, who have gone hence with the sign of faith, and now do rest in the sleep of peace. The closing remarks of the Rev. preacher were singularly beautiful, touching, and affecting; they prepared the mind for the service which was to follow, in which all the true children of God, however widely separated, and whether in the body or out of the body, do yet make but one Communion in Christ.

The sermon being concluded, there followed the administration of the Lord's Supper, the Rector acting as Celebrant. About 200 persons received the Blessed Sacrament; and thus the first service was happily and devoutly brought to an end.

At 3½ P. M., an informal meeting of the children of the Sunday Schools and Daily Parochial School of S. Paul's Chapel was held in the church. On this occasion many persons were present who had been, in past years, connected with these schools, as superintendents, teachers, or catechumens. The exercises consisted of a short service, the singing of hymns, and the delivery of brief addresses. The hymns were all taken from "Hymns Ancient and Modern;" those selected were, " *Blessed city, heavenly Salem,*" " *We love the place, O God,*" " *Jerusalem, the golden,*" and " *Now thank we all our God.*" The Rev. Dr. Haight gave many interesting personal reminiscences concerning the rise and growth of the Sunday School system in this city, and the history of S. Paul's School in particular. He was followed by the Rev. Samuel H. Hilliard, of S. Barnabas' House, and the Rev. Stephen H. Battin, formerly a scholar of this school. Lastly, the Rector distributed to the children an illuminated Memorial Card, designed for this purpose, and printed in many colors, by Mr. J. M. Kronheim. Each member of the schools received a card.

At 7½ o'clock P. M., a very large congregation was present, filling the church. Evening prayer was commenced by the Rev. Dr. Haight.

The sermon was preached by the Rev. Francis Vinton, D. D. The text was taken from S. Mark iv. 30, 31, 32, being the Parable of the Mustard-seed, and the subject was, "*The Church in Two Centuries.*" The following abstract of this very able, interesting, and important discourse has been furnished from a reliable source, and is printed in the shape in which it was received:—

The history of the Catholic Church, as foretold by our Lord in the Parable of the Mustard-seed, is verified also in the annals of the Protestant Episcopal Church, as a branch of the Catholic Church in this country, and especially in the biography of Trinity Church, in New York.

1st. The *planting* of the Church was, like the sowing of the mustard-seed—the least of all seeds—without observation, in the chaplaincy of military forces, in A. D. 1664.

2d. The *rooting* of the seed was a period of persecution and toleration of the Church. The phase of persecution extending to A. D. 1713; and passing thenceforward into the phase of mere toleration, until A. D. 1786.

3d. The *growing up* of the seed was evinced in the organization of the Church, through the consecration of the bishops, and organization of the General Convention, and the publication of the Common Prayer Book. This period may be characterized as the apology or defence. First, the defence of liturgical worship, as against the custom of extempore prayers; and second, the defence of the Apostolic Succession, against the claims of schismatic and unauthorized ministrations of the Gospel.

4th. *The becoming great* of the seed was when the Church proclaimed to her children their missionary obligations to our country and to the world, and her subsequent expansion into fresh dioceses.

5th. *The shooting out* of great branches from the seed was indicated by the consecration of foreign and domestic missionary bishops and by the Oxford tract movements, whence the souls and bodies of men were cared for, in preaching the Gospel and in works of charity. These characteristic times reach to this our day, in A. D. 1866.

6th. *The giving shelter to all*, that illustrated the full and perfect maturity of the mustard-seed, is marked in the history of the Church by

her provisions for ministering to the whole nature of mankind, by apply-
ing Christian art in subservience to piety, and subsidizing the beautiful
to adorn religion.

This may be named as the æsthetic era, when architecture and music
and the ritual claim particular prominence. In this complete aspect of
the Church we discover the operation of all the *spiritual forces* of the
former periods, just as, in the mustard-tree, the life of the seed pervaded
all stages of its growth unto perfection.

This is the glorious era on which the Church has just entered, and
which future annalists may note as contemporary with this celebration
of the Centennial of St. Paul's Chapel.

MONDAY, OCTOBER 29TH.

At 9½ o'clock A. M., there was a celebration of the Holy
Eucharist. The office was commenced by chanting Psalm
132, *Memento, Domine*, as the Introit, after which the Communion Service was said, as far as to the Prayer of Consecration, by the Rev. Dr. Haight, the Epistle being read by the
Rev. George T. Rider, A. M., of Poughkeepsie. The Nicene
Creed was sung, after the Gospel, to the 8th Gregorian; the
versicles, responses, and Amens throughout the service were
also sung. The Rector celebrated; and a considerable number of the faithful communed, including a number of clergy.

After the conclusion of the celebration, the church remaining
open, many stayed, enjoying the tranquil scene; and these
were joined by others, until, as the hour of noon approached,
a large assemblage was present again. There now appeared,
in addition to the members of the congregation, many persons who had in former years worshipped in S. Paul's, or
who had received there some rites of the Church; and among
these were some who had travelled long distances in order to
be present. So remarkable an assemblage of the old citizens
of New York, and persons interested in her history, has
never before, perhaps, been seen within those walls. The
reverend, the wise, and the venerable were there—the men
of past years with those of the present. The accommodations
within the chancel and in the church being limited, it had
not been deemed expedient to give special invitations to the
Centennial Services, except in a few particular cases; but a

general invitation, addressed to all persons "traditionally connected with S. Paul's," to revisit the church at such times as might be most convenient, during the three days' term, was cordially accepted, to judge from the number who came together to listen to the promised sketch of its history. The Rev. Samuel R. Johnson, D. D., and the Rev. John Brown, D. D., now for more than fifty years Rector of S. George's Church, Newburgh, were among the eminent persons present.

At 12 o'clock, the hour appointed for the delivery of the historical lecture, the Rector ascended the pulpit. The 103d hymn, "*From all that dwell below the skies*," &c., was sung to that grand old tune "*Duke St.*" The Lord's Prayer, and the collect, "Direct us, O Lord," were then said by the Rev. Dr. Haight; after which the Lecture upon the History and Antiquities of S. Paul's was read. The time did not permit the reading of the whole of what had been prepared: it will be found herein, however, printed in full, with the addition of notes and memoranda of great interest. When it was finished, the whole congregation united in singing the *Gloria in Excelsis*, after which they reverently received the Blessing of Peace. But long did they linger, broken into groups and dispersed throughout the church, exchanging salutations, conversing together about bygone times, and giving and receiving such pleasant and curious items of information as were suggested by a comparison of recollections, until, at length, this charming interchange of friendly sayings and not unprofitable observations came to an end, and the people reluctantly withdrew.

At 7½ o'clock in the evening, the Choral Service was sung for the first time in S. Paul's Chapel. The crowd assembled on the occasion was very great, the whole building being filled. The choir was a very large one, numbering about 60 men and boys, of whom the greater part were choristers of Trinity Church and Trinity Chapel, the whole being under the direction of Dr. William H. Walter, to whose industrious and laborious efforts the marked success of the two choral services was due. The staircase at the northwest corner of the church had been previously arranged as a temporary robing-

room; and, when the hour of service arrived, the procession
entered the chapel by the west door, in the following order:
1st, the junior choristers, some 40 in number, vested in sur-
plices; 2dly, the senior choristers, similarly vested; 3dly, a
select choir of Priests, in surplice and stole, consisting of the
Rev. J. I. Tucker, D. D., of Troy, the Rev. J. S. B. Hodges,
of Newark, N. J., the Rev. E. M. Pecke, of Riverdale, the
Rev. II. A. Neely, D. D., of Trinity Chapel, the Rev. W. H.
Cooke, of Lansingburgh, N. Y., the Rev. O. B. Keith, of
Jenkintown, Pa., the Rev. W. G. Farrington, of Hacken-
sack, N. J., and the Rev. George T. Rider, of Poughkeepsie;
4thly, the officiating clergy. The service was commenced by
the Rev. the Rector of the parish; the Creed and Prayers
were said by the Rev. Dr. Young. The following printed
memorandum of the order of services contains the particulars :—

. 1766–1866.

St. Paul's Chapel,

(NEW YORK.)

CENTENNIAL CELEBRATION

Monday Evening, Oct. 29, 1866.

FULL CHORAL SERVICE.

VOLUNTARY.

PROPER PSALMS, 68, 87.   .   (Trinity Psalter, pp. 125, 166.)

FIRST LESSON.

Isaiah, 45, 11–25.

BONUM EST. .   .   .   (Chant on p. 166, Trinity Psalter.)

SECOND LESSON.

Ephesians, 4.

BENEDIC, ANIMA MEA.   .   .   (Same Chant.)

HYMN 152.   .   .   .   "The God of Abraham praise."
(No. 253, "Walter's Manual.")

SERMON.

ANTHEM—Ps. cxxxii., 8, 9, 10. .   .   (W. H. Walter, 1853.)
"Arise, O Lord."

The Sermon was preached by the Rev. S. H. Weston, D. D., from Psalm cxi. 4—"The merciful and gracious Lord hath so done His marvellous works that they ought to be had in remembrance." The Rev. preacher addressed the congregation upon the subject of the Past and Present of S. Paul's Chapel. He regretted the want of statistics, by which he might have been able to give the whole result of what had been done during the hundred years through which the church had been open for divine service; the numbers of the baptized, the confirmed, the married, the buried, thus far; the bishops consecrated here, the priests and deacons ordained. Had these walls a tongue, what sermons would they preach, of the vanity of earth, the brevity and uncertainty of life, the unwritten history of so many individual souls! The preacher then went on to speak of the changes which have taken place in the lower part of the city, and gave some statistics of the churches and houses of worship which have been removed; in consequence of which removals not fewer than 120,000 souls are left destitute of the means of grace. He proposed to remedy the deficiency of church accommodation by holding more services in those buildings which still remain, thus making one church do the work of many, and also by constructing new ones of greater capacity, suggesting that we should put in more galleries, and borrow an idea from the places of amusement, public halls, &c., in which, as is well known, thousands hear better than hundreds can in some of the modern churches. It was also recommended that divine worship should be invested with all the attractiveness consistent with solemnity, decorum, and the reverence due to Almighty God; then, and not till then, may we hope to reach the masses of the neglected poor now perishing in our midst, under the shadows of our spires, and within the sound of our bells. "Brethren, let us do our part," said the preacher, in conclusion, "to hasten this consummation so devoutly to be wished; let us do our part to make the history of the next hundred years of this sacred temple as illustrious as the past. Time will at last crumble even these massive walls; but if, while they stand, they are a home for Christ's poor, the glory of the latter house shall be greater than the glory of the former, saith the Holy Ghost."

Mention should be made of the anthem, " Arise, O Lord," the chorus parts of which were admirably given, while the solos and duets were sung by the Rev. Dr. Neely and the Rev. Mr. Hodges. The duet by those priests, on the words, " *Let thy priests be clothed with righteousness*," was most devotionally and feelingly rendered.

The Blessing of Peace, followed by the full " Amen," closed this beautiful service; a " Sacrifice," indeed, to the praise and glory of the Triune GOD, offered with intense earnestness by thankful hearts, and fitly ushering in the commemoration of the morrow.

TUESDAY, OCTOBER 30TH. THE CENTENNIAL DAY.

A furious rain-storm from the southeast prevailed during the night of the 29th; but by 9 o'clock on the morning of the 30th all was clear, bright, and beautiful.

The first service held on this day was at 11 o'clock. Previous to that hour the altar had been dressed anew, with fresh flowers; and just before the commencement of the service there was received, by the Rector, a very beautiful cross of flowers, with the following note:—

" Will the Rector of Trinity Church permit this memorial cross, from the great-great-grandchildren of Rev. Dr. Auchmuty, Mary Auchmuty, and Allan Tucker, to be placed on the altar of S. Paul's Chapel.

" The Centennial, October 30, 1866."

The service was commenced by the Rev. Dr. Haight. The Psalms were chanted, being those appointed to be used at the consecration of a church or chapel—the 84th, the 122d, and the 132d. The Lessons also were taken from the Consecration Service, and were read by Dr. Neely and Dr. Weston. The Nicene Creed was chanted to the 8th tone. After Morning Prayer, the 52d hymn was sung; and, after the Gospel, an anthem from the oratorio of the Creation, " The marvellous works behold amazed," &c. The Rev. Edward Y. Higbee, D. D., Senior Assistant Minister of Trinity

Church, then ascended the pulpit, and read, to an exceeding-
ly attentive and interested congregation, the sermon preached
by the Rev. Samuel Auchmuty, D. D., in that pulpit, and
about that hour, just one hundred years before. Dr. Higbee,
before reading it, made some brief but impressive remarks,
with that good taste and peculiar felicity of expression which
are so characteristic of him, referring to the admirable qualities and faithful services of the venerable servant of God
whose words were about to be recited in our ears, and to the
presence of his descendants to the third and fourth generation. It seems proper to add a few words respecting the
sermon. The title-page is as follows:—

A

S E R M O N,

Preached at the Opening of

St. P A U L's C H A P E L,

IN THE

City of N E W - Y O R K,

On the Thirtieth Day of *October*, A. D. 1766.

By SAMUEL AUCHMUTY, D. D.

Rector of *Trinity-Church*; and Chaplain to the Right Hon.
William, Earl of *Stirling*.

Quifquis ades, tu maEte nova pietate, parumper
Exue mortales Curas, & te quoque Dignum
Finge Deo.

Publifhed at the Requeft of the Church-Wardens and Veftry.

N E W - Y O R K:

Printed and Sold by H. GAINE, at his Book-Store, and Printing-Office,
at the Bible and Crown, in Hanover-Square.

[Price, ONE SHILLING.]

2

To the sermon the following letter is prefixed :—

"To the HONOURABLE *Joseph Reade* and Daniel *Horsmanden*, Esqrs, Church-Wardens; And the other *Gentlemen* of the *Vestry*.

Worthy Sirs, In compliance with your Request, I now deliver you a Copy of my Sermon preached at the Opening of ST. PAUL'S CHAPEL.

IF in any Shape it may tend to promote the Glory of GOD, the Good of Religion, and a just Idea of the Sacredness of BUILDINGS dedicated to the immediate Service of ALMIGHTY GOD, which I am confident can be your only Inducement for desiring this Publication, I shall be most amply rewarded. But it will afford me an additional Pleasure, if what is now offered to the Public, may have any Influence in exciting others to follow so laudable an Example of Diligence, Benevolence, and Disinterestedness, as you have exhibited to the World, in the Undertaking, Conducting, and Completion of so beautiful and magnificent an Edifice.

THAT it may answer these important and laudable Ends, is,

GENTLEMEN,
The Sincere Prayer of,
Your Faithful Pastor,
And Much Obliged Servant,

S. A.

New York, Dec. 5, 1766."

The sermon is printed in small quarto form, 19 pages. The text is taken from Exodus, chap. iii., verse 5, "And he said, Draw not nigh hither. Put off thy shoes from off thy feet, for the place whereon thou standest is holy ground." The preacher, in arranging the heads of his discourse, undertakes to show :—

"1st. THAT ALMIGHTY GOD is eminently present in one Place, more than in another; and therefore, that such Place, with great Propriety, may be called holy.

"2dly. THAT CHURCHES dedicated to the ALMIGHTY's Service may be justly looked upon as such Places.

"From whence will appear—

"3dly. THE Obligations which we are under, while in such a Situation, and in the more immediate Presence of so holy a GOD, of behaving with Respect, Reverence, and Devotion."

The sermon is a fine specimen of the pulpit oratory of the 18th century; the arguments presented are drawn from Holy

Scripture, the Ancient Fathers, and the Divines of the Church of England; the style is clear, elevated, and impressive. The copy from which it was read bears the autograph of Aaron Van Nostrant; it was presented by the Rev. Wm. L. Johnson, D. D., of Jamaica, to his brother, the Rev. Samuel R. Johnson, D. D., Professor in the General Theological Seminary, to whose kindness the congregation was indebted for the pleasure of hearing again a discourse of which another copy could hardly be found.

The Holy Communion was administered to a large congregation, including some 30 or 40 clergymen, and about 300 of the laity.

The concluding service of the Centennial was held on Tuesday evening, commencing at 7½ o'clock. Like that of the previous evening, it was choral, the music being under the direction of Dr. Walter. The printed order was as follows :—

1766–1866.

St. Paul's Chapel,
(new york.)
CENTENNIAL CELEBRATION.

Tuesday Evening, Oct. 30, 1866.

FULL CHORAL SERVICE.

VOLUNTARY.

INTROIT—Psalm xxiv.   .   .   (Trinity Psalter, p. 52.)

PROPER PSALMS, 46, 48.   .   .   (Trinity Psalter, pp. 93, 96.)

FIRST LESSON.

Isaiah, 55.

CANTATE DOMINO. . .   .   .   .   ("Hodges in C.")

SECOND LESSON.

Revelation, 22.

DEUS MISEREATUR.   .   .   .   .   ("Hodges in C.")

HYMN 222.   .   .   .   .   "Hosanna to the living Lord."

("Chorals and Hymns," p. 72.)

SERMON.

ANTHEM—Ps. cxxii.   .   .   .   .   (Dr. Hodges, 1854.)

"I was glad."

HYMN 276.   .   .   .   .   "Jerusalem, the golden."

("Chorals and Hymns," p. 66.)

The following notice of this closing service was written by a person present on the occasion; and is inserted here as conveying the impressions of a very competent judge, and rendering unnecessary any other observations on the points touched on by the writer:—

"The concluding service of the Centennial Series at S. Paul's Chapel, on Tuesday, October 30th, crowned and completed the solemn climacteric of the three days in a memorable and fitting manner. For whether we consider the numbers in attendance, the excellence of the choral element, or the enthusiasm and earnestness of worship, nothing was more plainly manifest during this remarkable three days of public services than a climacteric spirit of zeal, fervor, and devotion, from the first to the last. And with a tender recollection embracing all of them, we do not hesitate to pronounce the final service queen of all the rest.

"From an early hour throngs filled the sacred building; indeed, it is almost doubtful whether, at any time during this privileged season, the church was at any time during the day or evening quite deserted. Worshippers found themselves strangely stayed to the sacred precincts. On this occasion, at the proper time, the choirs of boys, men, and priests, entered the church chanting antiphonally the 24th Psalm of the Psalter, passing through a standing and crowded congregation, and joining in the *Gloria Patri* when they had reached their stations in and about the chancel. The opening part of the service as far as the Psalms was devoutly intoned by the Rev. Dr. Neely, of Trinity Chapel. The Psalms (the 46th and 48th) followed antiphonally, with most stirring spirit, to single Anglican chants. The first Lesson was read by Dr. Weston, and the second by Dr. Higbee; while the *Cantate Domino* and *Deus Misereatur* were sung in full anthem to Dr. Hodges' familiar service in C. The Nicene Creed followed in unison on a monotone, closing with triumphant emphasis, as the organ harmonies came pealing and pouring in about the final sentences. The prayers were intoned very effectively by Dr. Haight, the *Amens* and responses being given with splendid precision and fervor by the great choir.

"Dr. Hodges' anthem, a well-remembered Consecration sentence, followed, in which the baritone solo 'I was glad' (originally written for him) was superbly given by the Rev. J. Sebastian B. Hodges. The Prayer of the three Priests in the same anthem, given by the Rev. Messrs. Cook, J. S. B. Hodges, and Dr. Tucker, all of the *Decani* choir, will long be remembered for its unexampled beauty of rendering and profoundly religious quality. Such vocal conjunctions, unfortunately, are almost as rare as the Pauline Centennials themselves. Then, after a few collects by the Rector of the parish, the Rev. Dr. Dix, came the ever-welcome *Jerusalem, the golden,* sung rapturously, and seemingly by every one, to its own glorious chorale, when, after the Blessing, the choir and clergy returned in procession to the vestry-room, the congregation remaining in their places."

It is not necessary to speak particularly of the sermon, as it was published in full in several of the city newspapers on the following morning. It contained a statement of the financial history and actual condition of the Corporation of Trinity Church; corrected some of those mis-statements which have been, and still are, rife respecting the value of the property of Trinity Church, its present and prospective income, and the management of the same; and sketched an outline of work to be done hereafter, for the temporal and spiritual welfare of the Poor in the lower part of the City of New York.

The narrative of the Three Days' Services being now completed, it remains to present, in full, with notes and illustrations, the historical account of Saint Paul's Chapel.

HISTORICAL SKETCH.

The work to be performed by me this morning is one of the most agreeable that could have fallen to my lot. A hundred years will have elapsed to-morrow since the first act of worship was offered, within these now venerable walls, to Almighty God. This is the Eve of the Centennial Day of S. Paul's Chapel; and you have been led hither through a feeling of affectionate interest in the sacred fane. A wish, or at least a readiness, to know more than you do at present of its history is, no doubt, generally felt; and as in foreign lands it is customary for a guide, familiar with the places resorted to by travellers, to accompany them from one shrine to another on their curious pilgrimages, and point out at each place the things most worthy of attention; so, on the present occasion, do I offer my services as your companion, proposing to draw aside with reverent hand the curtains which have veiled, for many years, the recorded annals of this sacred edifice, to exhibit, as among our most precious relics, this dear old church, and to recount the particulars concerning it which I have been able to gather from the lips of History, or from the less authentic, but interesting, reports of Tradition. It is gratifying to feel an assurance that the guide will have the attention and the sympathy of his audience, even though his task should be but imperfectly executed; for this old chapel holds so secure a place in the affections of good and true New Yorkers, that nothing which relates to it can be deemed unworthy of a hearing. The sole intact survivor of an era among the most critical in our history, and of which, in this vicinity, almost the vestiges are lost, it still retains respect in the eyes of an age which has made all things new; each year adds dignity to its form and outline, and each successive generation brings to these precincts the tribute of admiration and love.

The place at which we are assembled forms the verge of the old classic ground of Manhattan Island. Let me remind you of some facts which few among us remember. The City grew and extended itself, at first, along the East River: upon the western side of the island, for a long time, scarcely any progress was made. Thus it happened that, at the era of which I speak, some century or more ago, Broadway, above Trinity Church, was very thinly built, if, indeed, it could be regarded as built at all; it presented, on either side, a prospect of fields, orchards, and gardens, among which appeared at intervals the friendly outline of a public-house. This scarcely discernible street or highway, pursuing its vague course, terminated at length in a wide tract anciently known as "the Fields," and more recently as "the Common." That Common is now the City Hall Park. Originally the property of the States General of Holland and the West India Company, it was ceded, in 1686, to the Corporation of the City of New York, and remains to this day in their possession. In the early history of the Colony, it is conspicuous beyond all other spots. There the people were accustomed to assemble for the assertion of their political and civil rights; and many were the spirit-stirring transactions which occurred during the provincial era, on that debatable ground. The Common afforded ample room for such threatening demonstrations as were made, from time to time, by our forefathers, against the policy and measures of the ministry of King George III.; it witnessed a resistance to the Stamp Act as vigorous and persistent as that at Boston, and, if I mistake not, prior to it in time. Upon the Common, the "Sons of Liberty," as they styled themselves, came to blows, again and again, with the British troops, around a certain liberty-pole, which one party would cut down as fast as the other set it up: and there, in the year 1774, did Alexander Hamilton, though but a boy of

17 years, address a vast concourse of people, thrilling them by
the fire of his oratory and bearing captive their judgments by
the vigor of his thoughts. Such was the "Common," or "the
Fields;" a place upon whose outskirts, in one of the most
anxious and unquiet years of the history of the province, a
building began to arise, which was destined to remain the
sole survivor of an age now unregarded and all but forgotten.
The Common is still an open space; it bears, however, another name; and at this hour there is to be seen, of all that
once surrounded and adorned it, not one vestige, save the
brown walls, the portico, and lofty spire of this old church;
they still abide unchanged, in the position from which they
have observed, calm and motionless, the shifting scenes and
revolutions of this troubled world.

In the year of our Lord 1763, there was, on the line of
Broadway, and at the point where it struck the southern and
western edge of the Common, a field of wheat, which waved,
full bearded, in the breeze. On the 3d of November, in that
year, the Vestry of Trinity Church adopted an order or resolution providing for the erection of a second Chapel in the
parish, and fixing upon "the Church-ground on Broadway,
at the corner of Partition Street," or, as we call it, Fulton
Street, for the site. Thus, in that place where grew the
wheat, there came up in due time, from the generous ground,
a holy House, sacred to Him Who told us of His Mission in
the parable of the Sower, and called Himself the Bread of
Life. The order was given in November; materials were
collected, and it is said that the mortar was mixed, so that it
might be the harder for having stood some months before
use; and in the spring of 1764 the work of building was
commenced. The New York Gazette of Monday, May 14,
1764, has the following item of intelligence:—

"We are told that the Foundation Stone of the third English Church,
which is about erecting in this City, is to be laid this day. The Church
is to be 112 by 72 feet."

The autumn of 1766 saw it so far completed as to be ready
for use; and four days had yet to run of the three years since

the Vestry order for its erection was given, when the first service was held within its walls.

And here it may not be amiss to mention some facts in the general history of the Parish, which, although known to many of you already, may help others in forming a correct idea of the changes which have occurred. The services of our Church were first statedly held in a chapel inside a fort which stood near the Battery. The service of the Church of Holland had been performed there during the old Dutch régime. In 1664, when the Colony was surrendered to the British Crown, the rites and order of the Established Church of England were introduced in place of those which had previously been used there. Thirty-two years afterwards, A. D. 1696, Trinity Church was built, the Rev. William Vesey being the first Rector of the Parish.* On the 1st day of July, 1752, during the rectorship of Dr. Barclay, Saint George's, the first chapel of ease, was opened: in January, 1814, it was destroyed by fire, with the exception of the walls, which still stood; but in the following year it was rebuilt and restored. Dr. Barclay, having seen S. George's Chapel erected, formed the design of providing a second for the increasing wants of the people; he did not, however, live to carry out the project, which was accomplished, not long after, under his successor, the Rev. Dr. Auchmuty.

The architect of S. Paul's Chapel was a Scotchman, named McBean. Mr. Isaac Bell, who died A. D. 1860, at the advanced age of 92, was personally acquainted with Mr. McBean many years after the Revolution,† the architect being at that time a resident of New Brunswick, New Jersey. There are good reasons for supposing that McBean was a pupil of Gibbs, a man much more widely known. Gibbs was a Scotchman by birth, and a practical architect in London at the time of his death, which occurred A. D. 1754. He built that greatly admired church, S. Martin's-in-the-Fields, an edifice which S. Paul's so much resembles in the interior,

---

* See Note A at the end.

† See an article in the "Crayon" of June, 1857, from the pen of the Hon. Gulian C. Verplanck.

O This is the plan design'd for the New Church to be executed by Messrs Gautier & Willis

17th of July 1764.

Jos: Reade

Danl Horsmanden

George Harison

And^w Barclay –

Elias Desbrosses

FAC-SIMILE OF THE ORDER OF THE BUILDING COMMITTEE.

that there is no difficulty in tracing the ideas of the teacher in the work of his disciple, if, as seems highly probable, McBean and Gibbs held that relation to each other.

The builders are mentioned in a memorandum on an old plan of the Church; it is an elevation of the south side, and on the back this inscription appears:—

"This is the plan designed for the new church to be executed by Messrs. Gautier and Willis, 17th of July, 1764. Jos. Reade, Danl. Horsmanden, George Harison, Andw. Barclay, Elias Desbrosses."

These five gentlemen were probably the Building Committee of the Vestry.

In the latter part of the year 1766, a year memorable in the annals of the Province for uncompromising opposition to the Stamp Act by the citizens of New York, and for sanguinary collisions between them and the royal troops, this chapel was, in the main, finished: and on the 30th day of October, in that year, it was opened for the first public service. The New York Gazette of October 20th, 1766, contains the following notice:—

"On Monday, 27th instant, at 10 o'clock in the forenoon, the pews in S. Paul's Chapel will be let at public auction in said chapel, and on the Tuesday following the chapel will be opened, and a sermon preached on the occasion by Dr. Auchmuty."

The service, although fixed for the 28th, did not, however, take place until two days later. Then, with unusual ceremony, the new Chapel was formally opened. From the New York Journal and General Advertiser of November 6th, 1766, I take the following interesting and curious account of the scene:—

"Thursday last, the new Episcopal Chapel in this city called St. Paul's and esteemed one of the most elegant edifices on the continent, was opened and dedicated to Almighty God. The concourse of people of all ranks and denominations (who attended on the occasion) was very great.

"At 10 o'clk., the Council, Clergy, Church Wardens, and Vestry of Trinity Church, the Mayor and Corporation of the City, waited on his Excellency, Sir Henry Moore, our Governor, at Fort George. From thence they went in procession to the Chapel in the following order, viz.:

"I. The Mayor, Aldermen, and other Members of the City Corporation, preceded by the Charity Children of Trinity Church.

"II. The Clergy.

"III. The Governor's Council.

"IV. Their Excellencies Sir Henry Moore and General Gage.

"V. The Church Wardens and Vestry.

"After Divine Service, which was adapted to this particular occasion, an excellent Sermon was preached by the Revd. Doctor Samuel Auchmuty, Rector of Trinity Church. His text was taken from Exod. iii. 5, 'And He said, draw not nigh hither, put off thy shoes from off thy feet, for the place whereon thou standest is holy ground.'

"A suitable band of Musick,* vocal and instrumental, was introduced. Several pieces of Church Musick and psalms were sung and played by them in concert at the usual intervals; and the judicious Execution contributed much to heighten the solemnity. The whole was conducted with the greatest Decorum. The decent behaviour of the Audience, consisting of many Thousands of People, their devotion during Divine Service, and fixed attention to the Sermon, did Honour to themselves and to the Preacher."

Thus, with much reverence, this beautiful edifice, the pride and wonder of the city in its day, was opened and set apart for holy uses. And here it is in order to refer to that much mooted question, whether S. Paul's has ever been consecrated. There is no evidence that it ever had a consecration, in the full sense of the word. There was no Bishop in this country at the time when the Chapel was opened, nor until 18 years afterwards; and we have no intimation that any Bishop was at any time called on to remedy the supposed defect. But it must be observed that the Rector of Trinity Church was Commissary of the Bishop of London, and that, in the account of the opening services, it is expressly stated that they were adapted to that particular occasion, while in the Minutes of the Vestry (Vol. I., November 4, 1766) we find special mention of the ceremonies of October 30th as those of "the Dedication of Saint Paul's Chappell." Hence I conclude, 1st, that a consecration was intended, and, so far as

---

* As to this "Band of Musick," it appears that Sir Henry Moore made formal application to the Vestry for permission to introduce it, and that such permission was granted, not without hesitation, out of respect for him, and on condition that nothing unsuited to the solemnity of the occasion should be performed. —*Minutes of Vestry*, Vol. I., Oct. 29, 1766.

practicable in the absence of a Bishop, performed; and 2dly, that the proceedings had, constructively if not formally, the license and sanction of that Prelate who held in his jurisdiction the Province of New York. And now, having spoken of the erection of the Church, and of those ceremonies with which it was solemnly set apart for sacred uses, I shall proceed to review its subsequent history, and to mention some of the more memorable of the occurrences which have taken place here.

The years 1775 and 1776 were full of agitation in the Province and City. In the month of October, 1775, Tryon, the British Governor, terrified at the look of affairs, took refuge on the frigate "Halifax," and left New York, practically, in the hands of the revolutionists. Early in the year 1776, an American force, commanded by General Lee, and acting under the orders of Washington, entered and held the city. It was then that the Clergy of the Church of England closed their churches, on being forbidden to read the prayers for the King: to use the language of a contemporary, " the allegiance they had sworn to their lawful Sovereign, and an affectionate Attachment to his virtuous Character, compelled the Clergy to shut the Doors, rather than omit the dutiful Addresses which the Church enjoined them daily to offer to Heaven for his safety." S. Paul's Chapel remained closed for several months, during which time those events occurred which are so familiar to the student of the history of our revolution.* On the 14th of April, 1776, Washington arrived in New York, and assumed command of the American forces; and on the 29th of June Admiral Howe arrived at Sandy Hook with a fleet and transports bearing the troops to whom had been assigned the task of capturing the town. Then followed that disastrous campaign on Long Island, and the summer of reverses, the end of which saw the Americans in disorderly retreat and the royal arms victorious. On Sunday, the 15th of September, the British forces, under Lord Howe and Sir Henry Clinton, took possession of New York,

* See Note B at the end.

which remained from that day until November 25th, 1783, in their hands.

That same week, early on the morning of Saturday, September 21st, between 1 and 2 o'clock, the great fire broke out, in which about one-eighth part of this city was destroyed.* Trinity Church, the Rectory, and the Charity School, were among the buildings that were burnt. Saint Paul's was in imminent danger; its preservation was due, under Providence, to the remarkable energy and strenuous personal exertions of Dr. Inglis, the Rector of the Parish. On the following Sunday, September 22d, one week after the occupation of the city, and but one night after the fire, Saint Paul's was re-opened for Divine Service. The occasion was in all respects a memorable one. The preacher was the Rev. Thos. L. O'Beirne, Chaplain to Admiral Lord Howe: his sermon was printed at the request of the congregation. The title is as follows:—

"A Sermon preached at St. Paul's, New York, Sept. 22, 1776. Being the first Sunday after the English Churches were opened on General Howe's taking Possession of the Town and the Day subsequent to the Attempt to destroy New York by Fire. By the Reverend Mr. O'Beirne, Chaplain to the Right Honourable Lord Viscount Howe. Published by Particular Desire of the Congregation. New York, 1776."—pp. 20.

His text was taken from Jer. xii. 15, "And it shall come to pass, after that I have plucked them out I will return, and have compassion on them, and will bring them again, every man to his heritage, and every man to his land." The preacher was an Irishman by birth; he begins with an impassioned earnestness characteristic of his race:—

* "About one o'clock in the morning of the 21st * * * * a fire chanced to break out in a small wooden public-house of low character near Whitehall Slip. The weather had been hot and dry, a fresh gale was blowing from the southwest, the fire spread rapidly, and the east side of Broadway, as far as Exchange Place, became a heap of ruins. * * * * The wind veering to the southeast, the fire crossed Broadway, above Morris Street, destroyed Trinity Church, and the Lutheran Church, and, sparing St. Paul's Chapel, extended to Barclay Street * * * * of the four thousand tenements of the city, more than four hundred were burnt down. In his report, Howe, without the slightest ground, attributed the accident to a conspiracy."—*Bancroft's Hist. U. S.*, Vol. IX., p. 129.

"Was it then reserved for a Stranger to your Persons and your Altars
to address you on this happy Restoration of your Public Worship? This
solemn Re-establishment of your Religious Assemblies? Was it to have
been the good Fortune of One, to whom you were unknown but by your
Sufferings, to be among the first of the Ministers of God to bring the
Comfort and Consolation of his Word to an afflicted and persecuted
People?"

He draws a very graphic picture of the troubles of the
day:—

"Who that was a Witness of the cruel and disastrous Deed of the
Night before last, could promise himself that you should be assembled
this Day in the House of God, to praise Him for your wonderful Deliver-
ance? Who could have hoped that this Temple would remain a
Monument of the returning Favour of Heaven, amidst the Horror of the
Ruins through which you must have passed to approach it? Which of
you could have said to himself, that he should see those Doors opened
once more for the Reception of the Faithful, tho' as yet but as the
Shaking of an Olive Tree, and the Gleaning Grapes when the Vintage is
done? or hear these Walls, so long silent and unfrequented, filled again
with the Praises of him to whose Name you had raised them? Is not
this the Lord's Doing? Is not this our God for Whom we have waited?
We have waited for him, he hath saved us, and we will be glad and
rejoice in his salvation."

I must make one more extract from this sermon: the
words which I shall quote seem to have been uttered in
an almost prophetic spirit:—

"This has never been, and I am confident never will be, the Pulpit of
Contention and Strife. No Prophets, prophesying Lies in the Name of
the Lord who sent them not, shall ever turn it into a Stage for Sedition.
The Words of Truth and Life will never be perverted here in promoting
Violence and Bloodshed, under Pretence of consulting the Interests of
the God of Peace; to cause the Religion of the lowly, mild, and meek
Jesus to speak the Language of Ambition, Slaughter, and Revenge; or
to consecrate and deliver out in his Name the Sword that is to be
plunged by his Followers into each others Breasts."

These were remarkable words, especially when it is con-
sidered that they were spoken by a military chaplain to a
people intensely excited by alarm and passion. And how
marvellously have they been fulfilled, not here only, but
throughout our Church at large, which, sedulously avoiding

political questions, has confined herself to her proper work of preaching the Gospel, and ministering the ordinances of Divine Grace, and now stands united after the dreadful conflict of the civil war!*

Thus was this Chapel re opened; and for some years it held the position of the most important Church in the City. The ruins of Trinity remained untouched during the Revolutionary War; the grass grew in the crevices and the birds had shelter in the roofless walls; and for twelve years Saint Paul's served as the Parish Church. Meanwhile the struggle for independence went on, and the power of King George III., waning from year to year, declined towards that point at which the sun was destined to set in heavy clouds of disappointment and defeat. At last we find ourselves, after the passage of those stormy years, once more assembled in this Church; the day is April 30th, 1789, and the occasion is

---

* "Thomas Lewis O'Beirne, D. D., a learned prelate of the Established Church, and a native of the County of Longford, in Ireland, born in 1748. was descended from a Roman Catholic family, by whom he was sent to St. Omer's at an early age, together with his brother John, to study for the priesthood. In due course John took orders, and became a Roman Catholic priest in the diocese of which his brother was afterwards the Protestant Bishop. Thomas, on the contrary, renounced the Roman Catholic creed, and at the commencement of the American war, having taken orders, accompanied Lord Howe as chaplain of the fleet. On his return to England he published a vindication of his patron, whose conduct was at that time a subject of Parliamentary inquiry, and his connection with that noble family introduced him to the Duke of Portland. In 1782 he accompanied the Duke to Ireland as private secretary, and the following year obtained from that nobleman two valuable livings in Northumberland and in Cumberland. He was subsequently first chaplain to Earl Fitzwilliam, and was promoted to the See of Ossory, whence, on the death of Dr. Maxwell, he was translated to that of Meath. The writings of this popular prelate were, 'The Crucifixion,' a poem, 4to, 1775; 'The Generous Impostor,' a comedy, 1780; 'A Short History of the Last Session of Parliament,' 8vo, anonymous; 'Considerations on the Late Disturbances, by a Consistent Whig,' 8vo; 'Considerations on the Principles of Naval Discipline and Courts Martial,' 8vo, 1781; and several sermons and charges. He died February 15th, 1823."—*Blake's Biog. Dict.*

See also Croly's Life of George IV., for some very curious and entertaining incidents respecting O'Beirne. The author mentions a famous sermon preached by him in New York. and remarks that he was the only one connected with Lord Howe's conciliatory mission who brought back any laurels.

that of the Inauguration of George Washington, First President of the "United States of America."

The old Confederation had terminated, and the First Congress under our present Constitution assembled for the august ceremony. It took place at the City Hall, which then stood in Wall Street, at the head of Broad, just where the Treasury now stands. That building, a stately edifice in the Tuscan and Doric styles, known after 1789 as Federal Hall, and still remaining, in 1813, a rare old relic of other days, had been fitted up for the occasion, with many alterations and embellishments, under the direction of an architect and engineer named L'Enfant, of whom I shall have occasion to speak by and by, in connection with that strange piece of workmanship, the altar-piece of this Chapel. In the gallery of the City Hall, which looked on Wall Street, the oath of office was administered to the President, in the presence of what was called in those days "an immense assemblage of people:" he then proceeded to the Senate Chamber, and delivered to both Houses of Congress his inaugural address. After this the President, attended by the whole company, proceeded on foot to S. Paul's, to invoke the divine blessing on that nation which it had pleased Almighty God to call up on the face of the earth. Appropriate services were said by Bishop Provost, who had been appointed by the Senate one of the chaplains to Congress. At the inauguration of our rulers, scenes like that are no longer beheld: we have removed the ancient landmarks which our fathers set, and have declined to follow their reverent and religious example.

After his inauguration, Washington attended S. Paul's Chapel until Trinity Church was rebuilt. In his Diary, 1789 to 1791, as regularly almost as the Lord's Day comes round, we find the entry, "Went to St. Paul's Chapel in the forenoon." An interesting record occurs in that diary, under the heading of Monday, July 5th, 1790, as follows:—

"About one o'clock a sensible oration was delivered in St. Paul's Chapel by Mr. Brockholst Livingston, on the occasion of the day—the tendency of which was to show the different situation we are now in, under an excellent government of our own choice, to what it would have been if we had not succeeded in our opposition to the attempts of

3

Great Britain to enslave us; and how much we ought to cherish the blessings which are within our reach, and to cultivate the seeds of harmony and unanimity in all our public councils. There were several other points touched upon in sensible manner."—*Washington's Private Diaries,* edited by Lossing, p. 144. C. B. Richardson, New York, 1860.

Let us pass on, in our historical review, to the early part of the present century. Its first few years were years of great excitement and uneasiness, caused by the position which the British Government assumed on the Right of Search. The records of those days sound more like fable than sober fact. Incredible, and even absurd, as it now seems, English cruisers were in the habit of sailing up and down our coasts and into and out of our bays, of stopping and searching our trading vessels, and of taking from them whomsoever they chose to claim as subjects of the Crown. Thus, for instance, on Friday, April 25th, 1806, at 5 o'clock in the evening, a poor little sloop, laden with market produce and stores and hailing from the Delaware, was quietly making for the Narrows on her way to New York. Preposterously as it sounds to us, when off Sandy Hook she was fired into by a huge man-of-war of two decks of guns, bearing his Britannic Majesty's commission and named the " Leander." At the first shot, the little craft very submissively hove to. The frigate, however, fired again, and by this second shot, John Pierce, the brother of the captain of the sloop, who was standing at the helm, was instantly killed. When the sloop came up to the city, bringing the news and the corpse together, there occurred one of those movements which are prophetic of coming trouble. The affidavits of the captain and master, containing a full account of the outrage, were laid before the Common Council by the Mayor, and it was thereupon ordered that the funeral of the murdered man should take place at the expense of the city. At 12 o'clock meridian, on the 28th of April, the ceremonies were performed, in such a manner as to testify the depth and intensity of the public indignation. The body, having been taken from the City Hall, was carried in procession down Wall Street to Pearl, through Pearl and Whitehall Streets to Broadway, and up Broadway to St. Paul's. The flags on the shipping were

set at half-mast; all the bells tolled sullenly and ominously.
The corpse was preceded by the clergy in white scarfs, and
followed by the brother of the deceased and the hands of the
sloop; after them came shipmasters and sailors, and a great
concourse of citizens. The funeral service was read in St.
Paul's by Dr. Hobart, and the body was buried in the churchyard. The scene, no doubt, produced the desired impression.
When we read such stories in the records of the past, we com-
prehend better the principles which were involved in the
"War of 1812," and perceive the necessity laid on our forefathers of fighting it out as they did.

Pursuing the chronological order, we make our next pause
on reaching the year 1817. In that year the Lutherans celebrated the 300th anniversary of the commencement of the
Reformation. Similar commemorations had been held in
Europe, A. D. 1617 and 1717. The Evangelical Lutheran
Synod of the State of New York adopted resolutions in the
year 1815, inviting the attention of their synods and churches
throughout North America to the approaching jubilee. The
31st day of October, 1817, having been fixed upon for the
solemnities and exercises, they were held in the German language in the Lutheran Church in the forenoon, and in English,
in the afternoon of the same day, in St. Paul's Chapel, by
permission of Bishop Hobart. The Rev. Frederick Christian
Schaeffer, the Lutheran pastor, had the general direction of
the commemorative proceedings, which consisted mainly of a
musical performance and a discourse. In the forenoon Mr.
Schaeffer was assisted by the Rev. Mr. Milnor, one of our
own clergy, and the Rev. Mr. Labagh, of the Reformed
Dutch Church; in the afternoon, by the Rev. Mr. Mortimor,
of the Moravian Society, and the Rev. Messrs. Feltus and
Milnor, of our church. Tickets of admission were gratui-
tously issued; many thousands of persons, it is stated, were
present; and great numbers found themselves unable to
obtain access to the church. Mr. Schaeffer, in his account
of the solemnities, presents his thanks " to Messrs. Erben and
Taylor, to the gentlemen that constituted the orchestra, and
to all the ladies and gentlemen who in both churches assisted
in the attractive and excellent musical performances." .The

order of solemnities, in the German and English languages, was nearly the same. Mr. Peter Erben was engaged to superintend the musical performances in the German language, while the Handel and Haydn Society, under the direction of Mr. S. P. Taylor, conducted the music in the English tongue. The New York Historical Society, at a meeting November 11th, 1817, passed a resolution thanking Mr. Schaeffer for his discourse, and requesting a copy of it for publication. It was accordingly published by Kirk & Mercein, 93 Gold Street, together with a narrative, and a programme of the services, in pamphlet form, 12mo, pp. 56.

In the summer of the 12th year after that in which S. Paul's witnessed the obsequies of the murdered sailor, it was opened for another ceremony which fixed the attention of the entire community. The occasion referred to was that of the translation of the remains of Montgomery, and their interment beneath this chancel. General Richard Montgomery fell, as is well known, at Quebec, Dec. 31, 1775, in an assault on the lower town, and was buried near the spot where he died. The design of removing his bones to New York, long entertained, was successfully accomplished in the year of our Lord 1818. " After resting in peace for 42 years, within the walls and under the sod of this garrison," writes a correspondent of the " Commercial Advertiser," of July 7th, 1818, from Quebec, " the skeleton of General Montgomery was on Saturday last raised from its place of deposit and took its departure for New York, where it is destined to a more distinguished place of interment in the Church of S. Paul of that city." The coffin, when taken up, was found in complete preservation; the skeleton of the brave soldier was perfect, save the lower jaw which had been shot away. The remains were brought down under an escort of Revolutionary officers and a guard of regular troops; they were carried ashore at Fort Gansevoort, received by the Governor's Guards, and taken to the City Hall. On Wednesday, July 8th, 1818, the funeral took place. No scene so imposing had been witnessed since the funeral of Washington. The coffin was brought to Saint Paul's, under a military escort, followed by an immense procession; the pall-bearers were Colonel Varick

(President of the Cincinnati), Colonel Trumbull, Colonel North, General M. Clarkson, Colonel Willett, Colonel Fish, Captain Tiebout, and General Giles. The burial service was read by Bishop Hobart; and a brief eulogium was pronounced by Dr. Mason. The choral parts of the service were performed by the Handel and Haydn Society, while Mr. S. P. Taylor played the organ. The bones were laid to rest under that monument, with the aspect of which you are so familiar, and which had been previously erected to his memory by order of Congress.

Six years afterward, A. D. 1824, La Fayette arrived in the United States, having accepted an invitation to revisit the country which he had helped to raise from the humility of a province to the honor and dignity of a nation. His arrival and progress from city to city and State to State were attended by such demonstrations as might have better befitted a demi-god than a man, so exuberant was the joy with which he was again beheld, and so unbounded the evidences of attachment to his person. Indeed, on reading the narrative of that tour, the final wonder is that human nature could have sustained such fatigues, and that he ever reached his home alive. On the 16th of August, 1824, he landed at Staten Island; on the following day he came to New York. Among the tributes of respect shown to him, there must be mentioned a grand concert of sacred music which took place in S. Paul's, and at which he was present, attended by his suite. The notice of this entertainment is as follows. I take it from the "Commercial Advertiser" of September 9th.

"Grand Musical Performance. The Marquis de La Fayette has appointed to-morrow morning, at 12 o'clock, to attend the Grand Performances of the New York Choral Society in S. Paul's Church. An appropriate selection of Sacred Music from the best masters will be performed. James H. Swindells, Conductor. Tickets at One Dollar may be had at J. H. Swindells, 65 Bowery; W. N. Seymour, 6 Chatham Square; E. Riley, 29 Chatham Street; J. Cooper, 6 Maiden Lane; T. Birch, 235 Chapel Street, near Canal; of the members in general, and at the door of the Church from 10 till 12 o'clock. By order, T. Birch, Secretary."

While the subject of "grand musical performances" is

before us, let me observe, that oratorios were often given here in old time. Thus for example, to show how they were produced and with what favor they were received, it will be sufficient to refer to one, which was performed in the month of May, 1816. The " Commercial Advertiser " of May 27 announces it as follows :—

ORATORIO AT ST. PAUL'S.

The public are informed, that the Oratorio, which has been long in rehearsal, will be performed in St. Paul's Church, on the evenings of the 28th and 30th May. Tickets (3 dollars) to be had of Messrs. Eastburn, Kirk & Co., Messrs. T. & J. Swords, Mr. Peter Burtsell, and at Mr. Goodrich's Circulating Library, New York, and of Mr. A. Spooner, editor of the " Long Island Star," Brooklyn. Doors open at seven o'clock, and performance to commence at half-past seven.

Leader, Mr. GILLINGHAM.

Organist, Mr. S. P. TAYLOR.

The order of the performance for Tuesday evening, the 28th, will be as follows :—

PART FIRST.

Overture occasional	*Handel.*
Recitative—Comfort ye, my People	"
Air—Every Valley	"
Chorus—And the Glory of the Lord	"
Recitative and Air—O thou that tellest good tidings to Zion	"
Chorus—Unto us a Child is born	"
Solo—Violin, by Mr. Gillingham	*Viotti.*
Air—Total Eclipse	*Handel.*
Chorus—Then round about the Starry Throne.	"
Recitative—Ye Sacred Priests	"
Air—Farewell	"
Duett—There is a stream	*Trajetta.*
Grand double Chorus—He gave them hailstones for rain	*Handel.*
Air—Lord, remember David	"
Air and Chorus—Strike the Cymbal—accompanied by the six-keyed patent bugle	*Precetta.*

Second Part.

Overture—Sampson	*Handel.*
Chorus—Give to the Lord	*Trajetta.*
Air—Raptured Notes	"
Recitative and Chorus—Eloi	*Dr. Harrington.*
Dead March in Saul..................	*Handel.*
Air—Thou didst not leave his soul in hell.....	"
Chorus—Lift up your heads................	"
Air—O! had I Jubal's lyre	"
Duett—The Lord is a man of war	"
Grand double Chorus—The Horse and his Rider	"
Air—Let the bright Seraphim..............	"
Finale—Grand Hallelujah..................	"

To this advertisement another is added, as follows :—

ORATORIO

At St. Paul's, evenings of 28th and 30th May.

The Committee again inform the public, that the objects of the Oratorio are to aid in rebuilding Zion Church, and should the nett proceeds exceed $2,000, it is intended to present $500 to the Orphan Asylum. A generous public are requested to further the laudable objects of the Oratorio. A great expense has necessarily been incurred in order to "get up" the performance in becoming style.

Tickets, three dollars, to be had at Messrs. Eastburn, Kirk & Co. ; Mr. P. Burtsell, Wall Street; Messrs. T. & J. Swords, Pearl Street; Mr. A. T. Goodrich, Broadway; Mr. S. A. Burtis, Peck Slip; Mr. E. Riley, near the Museum, Chatham Street ; and Mr. Spooner, Brooklyn.

That the people who went to hear the oratorio were not ill pleased, may be inferred from the enthusiastic expressions of one who thus expatiates in the "Advertiser" of June 1, 1816 :—

COMMUNICATION.

Having been present at the Oratorio on Thursday evening, will you permit me, through the medium of your useful paper, to return those ladies and gentlemen, from whom I received so rich a treat, my sincere thanks. In the advertisements of the gentlemen composing the committee, they promised us something far superior to any thing we had heard of sacred music in this city ; and indeed they have fulfilled their engagements. The Choruses were well sung and played both in time and tune. The Double Chorus of the Hailstones was great, and repeated with wonderful effect. The Overture commencing the second part was sublime. The Solo of the Leader, Mr. Gillingham, was played with great taste and execution. But the Double Chorus of the Horse and his Rider exceeded every thing I could have imagined from the power of music to produce; and I declare it as my belief, that in no other city in the Union have the lovers of music ever enjoyed so rich a repast.

With this enthusiastic panegyric I might bring to a close the first branch of my subject, and, concluding the narrative of historic and secular transactions connected with St. Paul's, proceed to other matters relating to the structure itself. Before doing so, however, let me refer, though briefly, to one or two of the purely ecclesiastical services which have been held here, as standing forth conspicuously in the even line of the almost uninterrupted worship and devotion of a hundred years. Such was that memorable service which was performed on Friday, June 29th, 1787, when the first Bishop of New York was formally received by the Convention of this Diocese, in St. Paul's. After a long and tempestuous voyage, Bishop Provoost arrived in this port, from England, whither, as is well known, he had gone to obtain Consecration from the Prelates of our Mother Church; and being at length ready to assume the charge of the Diocese of New York, he was installed, by solemn induction, in that sacred and most responsible work and charge. Upon the day already mentioned, the Convention of the Diocese met, according to adjournment, and went to the house of the Bishop, where they were received by him. A procession was then formed in the following order:

1. The Charity Scholars.
2. Members of the Church at large.
3. Gentlemen of the Vestry of Trinity Church.
4. Lay Delegates of the Convention.
5. The Bishop and Clergy.

In this order they proceeded to St. Paul's Chapel. Upon their entrance, an anthem suitable to the occasion was sung by the Charity Children; the morning service was read by the Rev. Mr. Rowland; and there followed an address to the

Bishop, and his reply. (Journals of Convention, Dioc. N. Y., 1787.)

I shall refer to but one more service; it was held in St. Paul's on Wednesday, the 31st of October, 1832, during the session of the General Convention. The Rev. John H. Hopkins, D. D., Bishop elect of the Diocese of Vermont, the Rev. Benjamin B. Smith, D. D., Bishop elect of the Diocese of Kentucky, the Rev. Charles P. McIlvaine, D. D., Bishop elect of the Diocese of Ohio, and the Rev. George W. Doane, D. D., Bishop elect of the Diocese of New Jersey, were consecrated to the sacred office of Bishop. The Rt. Rev. Wm. White, D. D., was at that time the Presiding Bishop, and there were assembled, on that occasion, as his coadjutors, Bishops Griswold, Bowen, Brownell, H. U. Onderdonk, Meade, B. T. Onderdonk, and Ives. The Consecration sermon was preached by Bishop Onderdonk of Pennsylvania, from the text Isaiah lxvi. 21, "And I will also take of them for priests and for Levites, saith the LORD." The only Bishops absent were the Rt. Rev. Drs. Moore and Stone.

And now let us proceed to another division of our subject.

This church remains, substantially, such as it was in its first days; alterations have been made in it, but they have not changed its general appearance. For justness of proportion and elegance of style, it still holds a leading place among our city churches, and must be regarded as a fine specimen of its particular school of architecture. When it was built, the western end commanded an uninterrupted view of the river and the Jersey shores; for the waters of the Hudson then flowed up to the line of Greenwich Street; all beyond is "made land." The prospect must have been a pleasant one, and charming to the eye; we can imagine our forefathers, in those old days, grouped in the porch, before or after service, and standing still awhile to look down the slope of the green fields, and through the trees, towards the beautiful stream which rolled its waters to the bay. How often, of a still afternoon on the Christian Sabbath, when the day was declining, and when the skies were glowing above the Jersey hills with the golden light of sunset, may the

devout worshipper, in passing forth from the church, have
looked upon that fair appearance of gardens and groves, of
river and distant mountain, perhaps with a kindling fervor
of soul and a deeper realization of the truth that " there re-
maineth a rest to the people of GOD," or perhaps with the
melody of some old hymn floating through the spirit:

> " Sweet fields beyond the swelling flood
> Stand dressed in living green !"

How hard it is for us to form a correct idea of the ancient
aspect of these places ! King's College, erected in 1756, a
little to the north and west of this spot, on the block now
bounded by Murray and Church Streets, and College and
Park Places, was then quite out of town : it is described by
an English traveller of the period, as pleasantly situated near
the City of New York on the banks of Hudson's River.*
So stood the new church, beyond the city limits, away off in
the fields,† surrounded by groves and orchards, and hard by
the broad, bright river ; an object of surprise to the good
burghers, who scrupled not to comment with just severity on
the folly of that visionary set of men, the Vestry of Trinity
Church, who had put so large and ornate a building in a
place so remote and sequestered, so difficult of access, and to
which the population could never extend !

I have before me the original plans of the church : from
them it appears, that the portico at the eastern end formed
a part of the design ; although this has been, occasionally,
denied. And this may, perhaps, be the fittest point at which
to introduce the following carefully prepared table of dates ;
it gives, at a glance, the chronology of the edifice.

Nov. 3, 1763, order given for building St. Paul's Chapel.

May 14, 1764, corner-stone laid.

Oct. 30, 1766, first service held ; it being partially completed.

---

* See note C, at the end.

† A friend writes thus: "The late Mr. Robert Morris, of Fordham, West-
chester, told me he recollected walking into the country with my great grandfather from Queen Street, now Pearl Street, to see St. Paul's Church."

March 9, 1767, order given for carrying on the building.

Sept. 28, 1767, order given for finishing the Portico and fences.

May 14, 1781, churchyard ordered to be enclosed with a ditch and temporary fence.

May 13, 1793, report in favor of building a steeple at the N. W. end.

March 24, 1794, ordered that the steeple be built, after a plan designed by Lawrence, and then approved.

June 24, 1794, ordered that stoves be put in St. George's and St. Paul's Chapels.

April 11, 1796, a clock and bell ordered.

Feb. 13, 1797, a new roof to be put on.

July 22, 1800, an organ ordered from England.

Dec. 13, 1802, chandeliers ordered for the better lighting of the church.

May 10, 1804, a brick wall ordered to be built around the churchyard.

There was, at first, no entrance to the galleries eastward; but it appears that there was at the end of each gallery a room, communicating with it by a door. The room at the eastern end of the north gallery, although no longer in existence, deserves mention on account of its historical importance. It was known as the "Library Room;" and was so called, because certain books were kept there, which had been sent over, from time to time, by Bishops of London and by the Society for the Promotion of Religion and Learning, as gifts to the parish of Trinity Church. When the Revolutionary troubles began, other books belonging to King's (now Columbia) College, were taken to St. Paul's for safe-keeping and placed in the "Library Room," and subsequently, for the greater security of its contents, the room was stoned up, so that access to it by the door was cut off. Such, at least, is the tradition; and what makes it seem authentic is the fact that similar precautions were elsewhere taken for the preservation of property. I find, in the Vestry Minutes of April 11, 1780, an Order, that the Committee appointed for leasing the Church lands have power to employ proper persons to close up the doors and windows of the Parsonage and

School-house, and also of Trinity Church, to prevent the materials from being taken away. It must have been at or about that time that the Library Room was secured, as above described. The story goes, and several living witnesses concur in vouching for its truth, that many years had elapsed before the room was reopened, that the existence of the books had in the mean time been forgotten, and that their reappearance was the occasion of an agreeable surprise. However that may be, it is certain that the volumes were subsequently used by candidates for orders, and students of theology, and that, when the General Theological Seminary was erected in Chelsea, they were removed to the Library of that Institution, where they may be seen to this day.

And now I have to mention the great glory and honor of that ancient "Library Room." In it, the General Theological Seminary was born; or there, at least, the first children were nurtured, and thence were they sent forth. The Rev. Samuel H. Turner, D. D., late Professor of Biblical Literature in the Seminary, in a letter dated June 23, 1860, and addressed to the Trustees of that institution, on the occasion of the report of a Special Committee on the removal of the Seminary, writes as follows:

"I venture also to remark on another statement made in the same report in relation to the early history of the Seminary. Having been connected with it ever since its institution, and practically for more than forty-one years, I may be presumed to know the correctness of what I am about to say.

"The Committee make the following statement: 'The first seat of the Seminary was in the third story of a building in Fulton Street, opposite St. Paul's, afterwards removed to the upper room in the rear of St. Paul's, corner of Vesey and Church Streets.' If the Seminary ever had 'a seat' in Fulton Street, it must have been some time between October, 1818, and May, 1819, and solely under the instruction of Dr. Jarvis. I entered upon my duties the first of May in the latter year, from which time its localities were elsewhere. The original class was then limited to six. I have inquired of the four surviving members, not one of whom knows any thing of 'a seat in Fulton Street.' I have been told by one, that Dr. Jarvis began his course of instruction one month before I did; and by another, a resident then of this city, that he met the class in the vestry-room of Trinity Church. The removal afterward mentioned, to an 'upper room in the rear of St. Paul's, cor-

ner of Vesey and Church Streets,' must be a mistake. I feel very confident that there was no building then at that corner but a small one-
story engine-house. This I *know*, that, from the beginning of May, 1819,
to the end of the term, and from the commencement of the next term
after the summer vacation, until the weather became cold, Dr. Jarvis
and myself met the class *in a small apartment directly over the vestry-
room of St. Paul's, at the northeast corner of the church.*" [This was
the "Library Room;" and there the first class of the Seminary received
its early instructions from those good and learned men, Jarvis and
Turner, whose names will be ever held in honor among us. I add what
follows, for its interest, although it does not bear upon our subject.]
"Thence we removed to St. John's, where we had a fire. Some time in
the winter, we availed ourselves of the offer of one of the kindest and
best members of the class, to use, in the afternoon, a school-room at
the northwest corner of Broadway and Cedar Street, on the second
floor, where in the morning he taught a young ladies' academy. While
we were dependent for accommodation on this gentleman, who is now
a highly esteemed presbyter in the Diocese of Ohio, the Seminary was
removed to New Haven. On its subsequent reorganization in New
York, the classes were met occasionally in St. John's Church, afterwards
at the corner of Varick and Canal Streets, and lastly at the present
library room in the Seminary, until the west building was erected."
(Proceedings Gen. Theol. Seminary, Board of Trustees, 1860, page 356.)

In the letter from which I have given this extract, Dr.
Turner describes the Library Room as being at the northeast corner of the church, directly over the Vestry-room.
This is strictly correct, for the robing-room used to be at that
end of the north aisle; it was little more than a narrow
closet, lighted by the easternmost window on the north. At a
subsequent period, alterations were made; staircases were
introduced adjacent to the Broadway doors, and the rooms
above became mere vestibules or landing-places, by which
the galleries could be entered from their eastern ends. The
robing-room was then removed to the southwest corner of
the church, where it is at present; a staircase which formerly stood there and gave access to the south gallery was
removed, and two rooms, one above and the other below,
were thus gained in place of those which were sacrificed at
the other end of the church. But alas! for the change.
Ever since that time, the clergy who officiate here, must
make perforce a long perambulation, and literally "walk
about Zion" on their way to and from the chancel, much to

their own inconvenience and embarrassment, and greatly to the astonishment of persons unaccustomed to the ways of the place. Surely our fathers never intended this, nor thought of the penance which they were imposing on the timid and nervous—if any such there be—among their descendants.

The chancel remains as it was of old, the fitting place of rest for our large and stately altar, one of the best and grandest in the city; built at a time when queasy maunderings about "tables with legs" were yet unheard. The east window was originally of plain glass, and shaded with curtains; it has since been replaced in colors. And this brings to the mind the history of that marvellous altar-piece, by which the stranger's eye is instantly caught, and at which we, who are so well accustomed to it, still gaze with wonder as upon an object endowed with the power of steady fascination. I have spoken already of the death of Major-General Montgomery. In the year 1787, the Corporation of the City of New York asked leave of the Vestry of Trinity Church to erect in front of the great window of St. Paul's, a monument to his memory. Permission having been granted at a meeting held May 23d, in that year, the work was commenced and speedily completed. But since the new monument, standing against the window on the outside, and showing through, formed an unsightly object from within, the services of Col. L'Enfant were in request, to design something which might at once conceal the back of the structure and form a decoration for the chancel. A plan submitted by him was, on the 18th of June, accepted, and the order was given for its execution. Such is the history of our wondrous altar-piece; intended, as it seems, to symbolize, if not to represent, the giving of the law on Mount Sinai, it is perhaps as inappropriate as any thing that could have been invented to fill its present place; and yet I trust that the thought of removing so quaint and curious an object would meet with no toleration among us.

From the ceiling of the nave, and beneath the galleries, there once hung glass chandeliers, of curious workmanship; their only surviving representative now serves as a Corona in

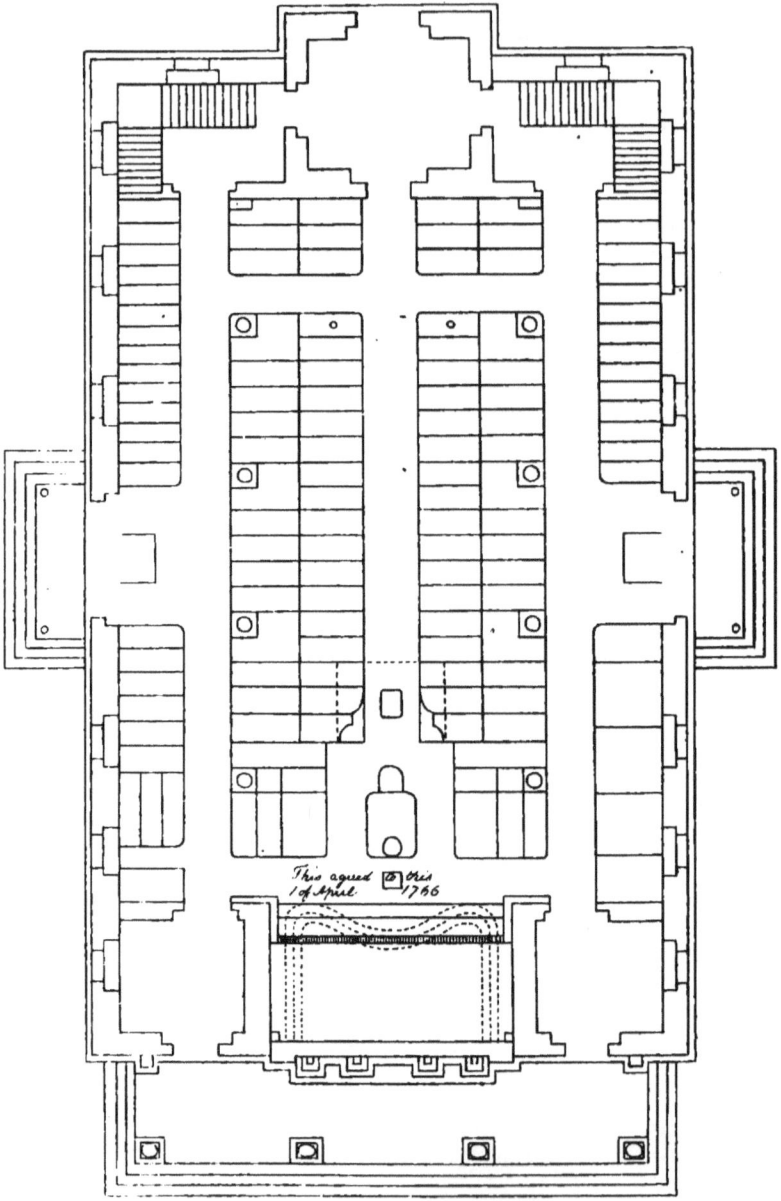

This agreed to this
1 of April 1766

the chancel. They were placed in the church A. D. 1802, and removed in 1856, when, for the first time, the gas-fitter invaded this old and classic scene. He plied, unmolested, his "dreadful trade," and the gas was first lighted on the second Sunday after Christmas, January 4, 1857.

But if we mourn our beloved chandeliers, in what terms shall we duly express our feelings as we think of those greater curiosities, of which not even a true representation is left, the President's and Governor's pews! It appears from the old ground-plan, a copy of which is here introduced, that the chapel had originally a north and a south door; these doors have long ago been filled up, but on the outside of the church their places can still be traced. It would further appear, that the north door must have been stoned up first, and that in its place there was made a canopied pew, elevated above the level of the pavement, and appropriately decorated and fitted up for his Britannic Majesty's representative and viceroy, the Governor of the province. The probabilities are that this was done after the destruction of Trinity Church, in 1776, when St. Paul's became the principal church of the city. After the Revolutionary War, this pew was occupied, no doubt, by General Washington, on the occasions of his visiting the church. But, as it was found inconvenient to have only one pew for the heads of the State and National governments, the Vestry took order for the preparation of a second pew, similar to the first and opposite to it. In their Minutes, May 13, 1785, the following record appears:

"*Resolved,* That the Committee of Repairs and Pews be directed to view the south door of Saint Paul's Chappell and report the practicability of shutting up the same and making in lieu thereof a large elevated Pew with two smaller ones on each side similar to the Governor's and the two pews adjoining, so as to make both sides of the church uniform."

The south door, accordingly, disappeared, and a second canopied pew took its place; and thus the chapel was provided with a President's and a Governor's pew. The canopies were supported by slender shafts similar to those under the organ gallery; and beneath them were hung the emblazoned arms of the United States and of the State of New York. Although no vestige of the pews can now be found, the old heraldic pictures have been preserved; they survived the destruction which, at some dreary day of modernizing and miscalled improvement, overtook the old seats of state; and were consigned to an obscurity which had this only advantage, that it kept them safe. At length, emerging from their concealment, they were hung up in the front lobbies, where for a long time they remained, until, some ten years ago, they were reinstated, as nearly as could be determined, in their old positions, where you see them now. It has been strenuously disputed whether the President's pew was on the north side or on the south. The facts which I have gathered seem to show that he sat, at different times, on each side of the church; on the north side, in the place of the Royal Governor, until the new place was provided, and then, for a short time, on the south; because, after the rebuilding of Trinity Church, it does not appear that he ever again attended St. Paul's. Yonder then is the place where Washington sat, with his wife, "Lady Washington," as she was called. There came to this church, some three or four years ago, an aged man, who talked to me at great length of those old times. He said, that when a boy, he used to sit with the school-boy tribe of that period, in the north gallery; and that the General and "Lady Washington" were wont to drive up Fair Street to church, on Sundays, in a coach and four; and that it was a never-failing delight to him and his comrades to watch them in the canopied pew below; nay, he said that he thought it a scene impressive beyond all others in this world, when they were there with all their state about them, while the dignified, elegant, and portly Provoost, first Bishop of New York, held forth in this pulpit as the preacher. But time has changed all this. Where now, throughout the land, are their own places set apart in church for the rulers of the people? And where is the reverence that formerly surrounded their persons?

As an interesting and valuable contribution to this portion of my subject, I insert the following communication from the Rev. John Brown, D. D., the venerable Rector of Saint

George's Church, Newburgh, who, in reply to a letter written at my request by the Rev. Frederick B. Van Kleeck, sent what follows :

NEWBURGH, Sept. 5th, 1866.

REV. AND DEAR SIR :—

I have received your note, making inquiry concerning the pew occupied by Gen. Washington in St. Paul's Chapel. There was formerly in that chapel a large square pew in the north aisle, adjoining the North Wall, called the President's Pew. Over this pew was a canopy supported by suitable columns. Against the wall was a painting in handsome frame representing the spread eagle with shield, being the coat of arms of the United States. Immediately opposite, on the south side, was a corresponding pew, with the coat of arms of the State of New York. This pew was called the Governor's Pew. Whilst I was acting as Librarian to the Society for the Promotion of the Gospel, these paintings were removed, and at my solicitation were placed in the Library Room, which was then over the north front door. When I left the city for a residence in the country these paintings were in the Chapel, and I suppose are there still. The President's Pew was without a doubt on the north side. Of this fact I am positive.

When Gen. Washington died I was not yet 10 years old, and do not remember to have seen him occupy the pew. But I remember to have seen him and Lady Washington enter the Chapel by the north door which led to the President's Pew.

Major Popham was asked during his life if he remembered seeing Gen. Washington receive the Holy Communion. His answer was that he sat in the north aisle near the President's Pew, and that Mr. and Mrs. Washington remained among the Communicants, and that he believed without a doubt that they both received the Holy Communion.

When St. Paul's Chapel was first erected, there was a door on the north and south sides. These doors, after the Revolution, were closed, and the President's and Governor's Pews took their place. Subsequently, when the pews of state were removed, the doors were stoned up and windows took their place. They are about the centre windows on each side.

Very respectfully yours,

Rev. F. B. VAN KLEECK.   JOHN BROWN.

Let me next proceed to speak of the organ. It is ancient, like the church, and has seen its vicissitudes. At a meeting of the Vestry, held July 8, 1799, a petition was read from sundry members of S. Paul's Chapel, requesting an organ for the said church; whereupon, a special committee was ap-

4

pointed to ascertain the expense of providing organs for S. George's and S. Paul's, and meanwhile the further consideration of the petition was deferred. On the 22d of July, 1800, authority was given to the committee to furnish, from Great Britain, organs for each of those chapels; and on the 12th January, 1801, the committee on leases was empowered to raise funds, by the sale of lots or otherwise, for the payment of the organs to be procured as aforesaid. Some time between this latter date and the end of the year 1802 the instruments must have arrived. They were made in London, by Mr. E. P. English. I find, that on the 13th of January, 1803, the organ committee was instructed to consider the propriety of placing ornaments on the organ! And that on the 10th of February following they reported adversely! What was it proposed to do? Was the organ to have been surmounted with figures of angels sturdily blowing through gilt trumpets? or what were the devices which were in contemplation by the over-sanguine progressives of the day?

Mr. Rausch was appointed, Dec. 13, 1802, to perform upon this unornamented organ, while Mr. Jackson was at the same time appointed at S. George's Chapel. The organists have been, Messrs. Rausch, Thos. Brown, W. Blondell, S. P. Taylor, Ed. Hodges, Mus. Doc., Wm. H. Walter, Mus. Doc., and M. K. Erben. About twenty years ago this instrument was furnished with pedals; two years ago it was not only renovated throughout, but still further enlarged and improved by the addition of a swell. And now, in its richness, clearness, and brilliancy of tone, it ranks among the most delightful and effective organs in the country: differing very much from those of modern construction, it impresses the intelligent listener the more by qualities peculiar to itself.

From the church the transition is not unnatural to the churchyard; thither let us betake ourselves; a few words will not be out of place concerning that sacred and inviolable spot. It contains not merely the bones and relics of great numbers of the departed, but also many monuments and headstones of more than common interest. High above all rises the obelisk sacred to the memory of Thomas Addis Emmet, bearing on its panelled base a memorandum of the latitude and longitude of the point on the earth's surface on which it stands (40° 42′ 40″ N., 74° 03′ 21″ 5 W. L. G.), and exhibiting on the north face a long inscription in Latin which few have had the patience to decipher. Close by it is a modest stone, lately restored by the Vestry with a reverent care which does them honor; it marks the grave of Philip Blum, Sailing Master of the " Saratoga," the Flagship of the gallant McDonough, who fought and won the battle of Lake Champlain. Nearly half way between the western porch and the school-house, beside the churchyard path, may be seen, enclosed by an iron railing, the monument erected by Edmund Kean to the memory of that renowned actor, Geo. Frederic Cooke; and somewhat to the south and west of it there stands a lofty tomb, bearing the name of a French soldier, E. M. Bechet, Sieur de Rochefontaine; he served in the War of Independence with the Count de Rochambeau in 1782, was appointed Adj.-Gen. of the French army in Saint Domingo, A. D. 1792, and afterwards entered and died in the service of the United States of America. This monument has also been in part restored, and since it has an historic interest, I add to this mention of it, copies of the inscriptions on its several faces:

On the West Face.

CI GIT
Etienne Marie Bechet
Sieur de ROCHEFONTAINE,
Né l'an 1755,
Dans le Canton d'Ay
en Champagne,
Département de la Marne,
Et décédé
Le 30 Janvier 1814
à NEW YORK.

Que son ame repose
Dans l'inaltérable paix
Du séjour éternel.

On the South Face.

E. M. Bechet
Sieur de ROCHEFONTAINE,
Se voua à la carrière des armes,
Et s'y distingua long tems.
Il fit, sous le Comte de Rochambeau,
La campagne d'Amérique,
Glorieusement terminée en 1782,
Par la prise du Lord Cornwallis,
Qui mit fin à cette guerre.
Louis XVI. le nomma en 1792
ADJUTANT-GENERAL
De l'armée de Saint Domingue,
Et après la mort du Roi,
Il entra Col. au service des Etats Unis.
Enfin il se retira en 1798,
Pour jouir au sein de l'amitié,
D'une considération justement acquise,
Et d'un repos dignement mérité.

On the North Face.

CE TOMBEAU
Qu'a fait ériger
Made. Catherine Gentil
A LA MEMOIRE
D'un digne et vertueux Père,
N'est point l'orgueilleux ouvrage
D'une vanité mondaine,
C'est un Monument consacré
Par la Piété Filiale.
Puissent les vœux d'une pieuse Fille
S'élever jusqu'au trône
Du tout-puissant,
Et attirer la miséricorde divine
Sur le respectable objet
De ses douloureux regrets.

On the East Face.

O vous qui visitez dans un saint recueillement
Ce silencieux asile

DES MORTS
Joignez vos vœux
A ceux d'une pieuse Fille,
Et priez avec elle
Pour le repos de l'ame
de Feu
Mr. E. M. Bechet,
Sieur de Rochefontaine.

Inside the church there are many tablets, of more or less interest. Six of these are inserted in the walls of the chancel, bearing the names, respectively, of Colonel Thomas Barclay, son of the Rev. Henry Barclay, D. D., and some time British Consul at New York; of Margaret, wife of the Rev. Charles Inglis, D. D., some time Rector of Trinity Church and Bishop of Nova Scotia; and of Sir John Temple, Bart. These tablets are on the north side of the chancel, and have the arms of the respective families emblazoned on them in colors. On the opposite wall are the tablets, similarly decorated, of Anthony Van Dam, son of the Hon. Rip Van Dam; of Elizabeth Franklin, wife of his Excellency William Franklin; and of a lady named Eleonora Hugget, whose qualities and character are thus celebrated:

" Sub hoc Marmore positæ sunt exuviæ
Eleonoræ, uxoris Sigismundi Hugget
De Nova Eboracensi Armigeri,
Natæ Lincolniensi urbis Magnæ Britanniæ:
Cujus si indefessam in Deum pietatem,
Immotam in amicos fidem,
Amorem ad maritum illibatum,
Si in æquales comitatem,
In egenos liberalitatem,
In omnes spectes benevolentiam,
Vix hæc ætas parem habuit,
Superiorem nulla.
Obiit III. Men. Decem. MDCCXCV. Ætatis LVII."

Of all the monuments within the church, the loftiest and most conspicuous is that erected to the memory of John

Wells; it stands at the west end, and has a long inscription, and a bust of that eminent jurist and counsellor.

But in speaking of the monumental stones in or about S. Paul's, I must not omit to mention that one which is apparently the oldest of them all, or rather the oldest in the country, or even in this hemisphere. It bears date A. D. 1084, and has been visited by multitudes who were curious to see so remarkable an object. What other churchyard in the land can boast a stone nearly coeval with the Norman Conquest? It may be found on the north side of the ground, about three-quarters of the way westward from the front line of the porch, and very near the railing. "Siste Viator," may we exclaim; pass not by, till you have seen what you never saw before, and perhaps may never see again.*

In the memorandum of dates given some pages back, it is shown that the burial-ground, originally an open plot, was, in 1781, enclosed with a ditch and temporary fence, and that in 1804 it was better protected by a low brick wall; the iron railing which now surrounds it is of comparatively recent date. Long ago, the cattle used to stray into the church-yard, and browse among the monuments; nay, there is an old tradition, that once upon a time, while Divine service was going on, perhaps of a warm and pleasant summer's afternoon, a horse came into church and walked some distance up the middle aisle. In his rambles, he had strayed into the churchyard; his attention had then been turned to the shady porch and open door; and, meeting with no discouragement from sexton, churchwarden, or similar official, he had proceeded on his tour of investigation, and thus had made his appearance among the worshippers, to their extreme surprise, and to his ultimate discomfiture.†

---

* It is true that there are some who surmise, if they do not actually allege, that the stone is not so old as it seems to be, and who have invented the theory that the stonecutter has transposed an 8 and an 0; but these are the captious objections of that school which delights in finding solutions for every thing mysterious, and in whose eyes the most venerable things are often held cheap, and treated with unseemly freedom.

† A lady present at the delivery of this lecture, assured me afterwards that this incident was true, and that she knew, personally, that the horse did so

I have spoken already of a narrow escape of the chapel from destruction by fire in the year 1776. It was in similar peril in 1799 ; the fire was in Vesey Street, and the steeple was actually in flames. It appears that on this occasion sev- eral persons rendered important aid, for the Vestry appro- priated $150 to be distributed to the most active in putting out the fire (Minutes, vol. i., April 22, 1799). Two years afterwards (March 9, 1801), we find a claim put in by one John White, who thought that he deserved compensation for services rendered, and up to that time unrewarded, and accordingly the Vestry made him a grant of $30 for what he did, a sum which fell $20 short of that which he had named as, in his judgment, not beyond his deserts. Other fires, en- dangering the church, occurred in 1820 and in 1848, when, for the first and second times, the Park Theatre was burnt. But never, perhaps, did S. Paul's go through a more trying ordeal than on the 13th July, 1865. On that well remem- bered day, about half an hour after noon, a fire broke out in Ann Street, which very soon extended to the American Museum. That immense building, little more than a gigan- tic packing-box of light inflammable stuff, was, in an incred- ibly short space of time, a mass of living fire. It hap- pened that I was on the spot, and saw the beginning of the conflagration. Going to the portico on Broadway to observe the progress of events, I remained there until we were driven out by the intolerable heat ; and as it became evident that the church was in imminent danger, I ascended to the roof, with several persons, and remained there until half-past four in the afternoon. Those were hours of intense anxiety ; but under Divine protection the peril was again averted, and the church, though badly scorched and defaced, was saved. To this happy result two causes mainly contributed. The wind, when the fire broke out, was so light, that the smoke ascended

---

enter as described. She writes thus: "In my childhood I frequently heard my great aunts (the Misses Ludlow) relate the tale of the horse walking up the aisle of St. Paul's Church, during the service, to say his prayers. They said there were no fences round the churchyard in those days, and they looked upon it as a walk into the country from their house in Hanover Square, which was a part of Queen Street, now called Pearl."

almost in vertical column to the sky; soon, however, the breeze freshened, but in doing so it shifted some six or seven points until it came out from the N. W. Had it blown from S. or E., no human exertions could have saved the church. But, 2dly, I must mention the efforts of the generous and devoted firemen, and others, as contributing to our escape. Then for the first time did I realize how strong a hold this venerable edifice has on the affections of all classes of our townsmen; since I was beset by volunteers who enthusi astically offered their services to do any thing they could, in that emergency; their honest and hearty expressions cannot be forgotten. Among them was a man who gave me his name as Captain de Rohan, an old officer of Garibaldi's army. His services were accepted; he worked hard all day, and kept watch all the following night; he would receive no compensation, and scarcely even thanks. And he was but one of many whose services are hereby gratefully acknowledged

It would no doubt be possible to add considerably to the reminiscences of Saint Paul's Chapel; and this may yet be done hereafter by some other hand. At this point, however, I shall bring my task to a close; a task which has certainly been fulfilled *con amore*, if not as well as I could desire. But enough has been collected to show the value and importance of this historic relic, and to invest it with a deeper interest in the eyes of our citizens, many of whom now hear, for the first time, the records of its fame. If, however, it be entitled to the reverence of the antiquary and the lover of ancient things, how should I undertake to express those deeper emotions with which it must be regarded by the religious mind? Veneration for old things is a quality too seldom found in the characters of our countrymen; their wont is, to disparage the judgment and wisdom of the past, to remove what reminds us of our forefathers, and to lay the ancient landmarks even with the dust. When, therefore, men gather about some one of those bequests of the past with a view not to demolish, but to protect it, when they bestow some care and pains (though but a little) in keeping safe from destruction some waif from the flood of time, they

render, unless we mistake, a positive service to their generation, and help to elevate the tone of the community. Such
an office is ours; and to it we add another; since our work is
one, not merely of filial respect and piety, but of Christian
and religious duty. The object which we hold so dear, and
of which we are keeping the 100th birthday, has a double
sacredness; not that alone which hoary years confer, but
that older and more awful sanctity imparted, by the Divine
possession, to the instruments wherewith GOD acts on man.
As citizens, and as Christians, therefore, we are doing that
which is lawful and right, what is expedient, and also what
is just. And may Almighty GOD bless and accept this service! Long may this Church stand! GOD forbid that any
eye should witness its destruction or removal, though twice
or thrice a hundred years should have rolled away! So
long as New York shall stand, so long stand S. Paul's,
beloved and cared for of GOD and of man, wearing the palm
and honors of a hale and green old age, and of a fair and
worthy history, and having around it the daily growing
brightness of a divine and sacred light.

NOTES.

NOTE A.

DR. BERRIAN, in his History of Trinity Church (page 23), makes the following statement concerning the Rev. Mr. Vesey:

"The new Rector first performed divine service in Trinity Church, on the 6th of February, 1697."

This is a mistake. Mr. Vesey was not ordained until August of that year, and his first service was held March 13, 1698, as appears from documents in the Surrogate's office in the city of New York, and from the Minutes of the Vestry. The documents may be found in the "Record of Will, No. 2, 1682 to 1692," pages 100–104, from which I have transcribed them with care, and here present them in full, as forming an interesting and important item in the history of the parish.

"These following papers were recorded at the request of Mr. William Vesey, Rector of Trinity Church in New York.

"TENORE p̄sentium Nos HENRICUS permissione Divina LONDINENSIS EPISCOPUS notum facimus universis, quod die secundo Mensis augusti Anno Dom. millesimo sexcentessimo nonagesimo septimo in Capella nostra intra pallatium nostrum de Fulham Middlesexiæ, nos p̄fatus HENRICUS LONDINENSIS EPISCOPUS antedictus sacros ordines Dei omnipotentis p̄sidio celebrantes: Dilectum Nobis in Christo Gulielmum Vesey A. M. ex universitate Oxoñ de vita sua Laudabili ac morum et virtū̄m suarum donis Nobis multipliciter Comendatum ac in Bonarum Liturarum studio et scientia Eruditum et per nos et alios quo ad omnia in ea parte requisita examinatum et approbatum in Sacrum Diaconatus ordinem juxta morem et ritum Ecclesiæ Anglicanæ in hac parte salubriter editos et provisos admisimus et promovimus Ipsumque in Diaconum Rite et Canonice tunc et ibidem ordinavimus. IN CUJUS REI TESTIMONIUM Sigillum Nostrum Episcopale presentibus apponi fecimus. Datis die et anno p̄dictis Nostraeque translationis anno vicesimo secundo. H. LONDON."

"TENORE p̄sentium Nos HENRICUS permissione Divina LONDINENSIS EPISCOPUS notum facimus universis, quod die secundo Mensis augusti Anno Dom. millesimo sexcentessimo nonagesimo septimo in Capella nostra intra pallatium nostrum de Fulham Middlesexiæ, nos pfatus HENRICUS LONDINENSIS EPISCOPUS antedictus sacros ordines Dei omnipotentis p̄sidio celebrantes: Dilectum Nobis in Christo Gulielmum Vesey A. M. ex universitate Oxoñ de vita sua Laudabili ac morum et virtū̄m suarum donis Nobis multipliciter Comendatum ac in Bonarum Liturarum studio et scientia Eruditum et per nos et alios quo ad omnia in ea parte requisita examinatum et approbatum in Sacrum Presbyteratus ordinem juxta morem et ritum Ecclesiæ Anglicanæ in hac parte salubriter editos provisos admisimus et promovimus Ipsumque in Presbyterum Rite et Canonice tunc et ibidem ordinavimus. IN CUJUS REI TESTIMONIUM Sigillum Nostrum Episcopale presentibus apponi fecimus. Datis die et anno p̄dictis Nostraeque translationis anno vicesimo secundo. H. LONDON."

"HENRY, by divine permission LORD BISHOP OF LONDON, To all to whom these presents Shall or may consern, health in our Lord God everlasting.

WHEREAS, by an act of Parliament made in the first year of our Sovereign Lord and Lady King WILLIAM and Queen MARY, Entitled an act for the abrogating of the oaths of Supremacy and Allegiance and appointing other oaths, it is provided and Enacted that Every person, at his or their respective admission to be incumbent in any Ecclesiastical promotion or dignity in the Church of England shall subscribe and declare before his ordinary in manner and form, as in the sd. act is contained Now Know Ye, that on the day of the date hereof, did personally appear before us, Mr. William Vesey to be admitted to the Ministeriall function in ye

II. London.
City of New Yorke, and subscribed as followeth, as by the said act is required. I William Vesey do declare that I will Conform to the Liturgy of the Church of England as it is now by law established. In witness whereof we have caused our seale manual to be affixed to these presents, Dated the second day of August, in the year of our Lord one thousand six hundred Ninety-Seaven, and in the 22d year of our Translation."

"Henricus permissione Divina Londinensis Episcopus Dilecto Nobis in Christo Gulielmo Vesey clerico Salutam et Gratiam: ad peragendum Officium parochi in Eclesia de New Yorke in partibus occidentalibus in presibus Communibus aliisque Ministeriis Ecclesiasticis ad officium parochi pertinentibus, juxta formam descriptam in Libro publicarum precum authoritate parliamenti hujus Inclyti Regni Angliæ in ea parte edit. et provis. et Canones et Constitutiones in ea parte Legitime Stabilitas et publicatas et non aliter neque alio modo tibi de cujus fidelitate morum Integritate, Literarum Scientia, Sana Doctrina et Diligentia plurimum confidimus (prestito primitus per te Iuramento

H. London.
tam de agnosendo regiam Supremam Majestatem Juxta vim, formam et Effectum Statuti parliamenti dicti regni Angliæ in ea parte edit. et provis. quam de Canonica Obedientia Nobis et Successoribus nostris in omnibus licitis et honestis per te prestanda et exhibenda Subscriptisque per te Tribus illis Articulis mentiónatis in Tricessimo Sexto Capitulo Libri Constitutionum sive Canonum Ecclesiasticorum anno Domini 1604 regia authoritate Editorum et promulgatorum) Licentiam et facultatem Nostram Consedimus et Impertimur per presentes ad Nostrum beneplacitum Duntaxit Duraturas. In cujus Rei Testimonium Sigillum Nostrum quo in similibus plerumque utimur presentibus apponi fecimus."

"Dat. secundo die Augusti, 1697."

"By His Excelly. Coll. Benjamin Fletcher, Capt., Genll., and Govr. in Chief of the Province of New York, &c.

"These are to certifie unto all to whom these presents shall come or may Consern, that on Sunday, the 13th of March Instant, at the first opening of Trinity Church in New Yorke, after ye reading the Morning and Evening Service, Mr. William Vesey did declare before his Congregation his unfeigned assent and consent to all and everything contained and prescribed in, and by the book Entituled the book of Comon prayer, and administration of the Sacraments and other rites and Ceremonies of the Church, according to the use of the Church of England, together with the Salter, or psalms of David, pointed as they are to be sung or said in Churches in the form and manner of making, consecrateing, and ordaining and consecrateing of bishops, priests and Deacons, and in the Time of divine service did read a certificate from the Rt. Reverend father in God, Henry Lord Bishop of London that he had subscribed the acknowledgment or Declaration according to the act of uniformity.

"In Testimony whereof I have hereunto Sett my hand seale at New York the 25th of March, Annoque Domini, 1698. Ben. Fletcher."

From the Minutes of the Vestry of Trinity Church we get further light on the subject of the opening of the church for divine service. The meeting at which the Rev. Mr. Vesey's name first occurs as present, was held Monday, January 31st, 1698. At that meeting the following order was adopted:

"*Ordered*, That Trinity Church be cleared to-morrow, Divine Service being to be read therein the next Sunday. Mr. Jeremiah Tothill having accepted to oversee the performance thereof, this board promising to refund him in the expense thereon."

It appears, however, that the doors were yet unfinished, that the windows were still unglazed, and that the pulpit had not been set up; so that it could not be got ready. After a delay of more than a month, another resolution was adopted on Monday, March 7, 1698, as follows:

"*Ordered*, That Capt. Thos. Clarke, Mr. Wm. Huddleston, and Mr. John Crooke do take care that the Church be cleared and put into the best posture they can in order that Divine Service and the Communion be there administered the next Sabbath day."

The next Sunday was March 13, and Gov. Fletcher's certificate shows that on that day the Church was opened, and that the rector officiated there for the first time.

Dr. Berrian's error is accounted for, as to the day of the month, by his supposing that the order of Jan. 31st was carried out, and as to the year (which he makes 1697 instead of 1698), by the fact that he was misled by a clerical error; for in the transcription of the Minutes, the copyist has carried the date 1697 into the year 1698, as far as to March 26th, when it would appear that he discovered his mistake, but did not take the trouble to go back and correct it, fearing, perhaps, to spoil the looks of his beautiful penmanship by erasures.

NOTE B.

The following communication has been received from Miss Auchmuty, of Washington, D. C., a grand-daughter of Dr. Auchmuty, and is inserted with much pleasure, as an authentic contribution to the history of the times; the writer says:

"I write what I have heard from earliest childhood were the incidents related. It may not be uninteresting to Trinity Parish, which has, in the centennial celebration of St. Paul's, done so much honor to the memory of my grandfather, to know why he was led to leave New York when all his best feelings prompted him to remain with the devoted flock, to whom he was a faithful pastor.

"In the most serious times of the Revolutionary War, when the Americans took possession of New York, Dr. Auchmuty's position as Rector of Trinity Church caused him to be a peculiar mark for the persecution to which the clergy and loyalists generally were subjected, by a people regardless of aught but their zeal to relieve their country from the sway of England; and he had necessarily much to endure, in consequence of what were deemed his obnoxious principles. On two or three occasions Dr. Auchmuty had been forbidden by the authorities to use the prayers for the king; but nothing would induce him to swerve from his decision to read the service in the usual form.

"The students of King's College, and a number of his friends, having understood that violence might be anticipated, went to church in order to protect him, should it be necessary. After service, Dr. Auchmuty held a consultation with his vestry, when they delivered to him the keys of Trinity, St. Paul's, and St. George's, which he took, saying that 'the house of God must no longer be subjected to desecrations;' and with the promise to return to his flock as soon as they could be permitted to worship without molestation, he went into the Jerseys (as New Jersey was then called) to the protection of the British lines.

"When the English again took possession of New York, he applied to General Washington for a pass through the American lines, that he might be enabled to return to his charge. This was refused; but not daunted thereby, Dr. Auchmuty determined to make the attempt to return without it. By walking through the woods at night, at the expiration of a week his painful journey was accomplished, and he reached his beloved flock only to find the church he so venerated burnt to the ground, with the parsonage attached to it, and the valuable archives mostly destroyed.

"With a heart overwhelmed with sorrow, he preached twice in St. Paul's Church on the Sunday after his return, and the following week was taken ill with erysipelas, brought on by the exposure and fatigue he had just undergone. He died within a few days afterwards, and his remains were placed beneath the chancel of St. Paul's.

"His life was thus cut off in its full vigor, and in the midst of his usefulness— a martyr in the cause of the Church, in whose service that life had scarce been spent."

NOTE C.

Although it is not directly connected with the subject, the reader may not take it amiss if I present the following copy of verses written by Dr. Cooper, once President of Columbia College. A strong maintainer of the Royal prerogative, he became so odious to the people, that on the 10th of May, 1775, they attacked the College, and would no doubt have taken his life, if he had not been so fortunate as to escape in the darkness. These lines were written by him on the anniversary of that day, May 10th, 1776, when he was safe in England; they contain an account of his precipitate flight. Note especially what the good Doctor writes respecting the "*sounding shore*" of the Hudson, and its "*beach*," along which he wandered in great and just alarm:

To thee, O God! by whom I live,
The tribute of my soul I give,
   On this revolving day.
To thee, O God! my voice I raise,
To thee, address my grateful praise,
   And swell the duteous lay.
Nor has his orb unceasing run
Its annual circle round the sun,
   Since when the heirs of strife,
Led by the pale moon's midnight ray,
And bent on mischief, wend their way
   To seize my guiltless life.
At ease my weary limbs were laid,
And slumbers sweet around me shed
   The blessings of repose,
Unconscious of the dark design,
I knew no base intent was mine,
   And therefore feared no foes.
When straight a Heaven-directed youth,*
Whom oft my lessons led to truth
   And honor's sacred shrine,
Advancing quick before the rest,
With trembling tongue my ear addrest,
   Yet sure in voice divine.
"Awake! awake! the storm is nigh,

---

* Mr. Nicholas Ogden.

This instant rouse—this instant fly,
　　The next may be too late;
Four hundred men, a hostile band,
Access importunate demand,
　　And shake the groaning gate."
I wake—I fly—whilst loud and near,
Dread execrations wound my ear,
　　And sore my soul dismay.
One avenue alone remain'd,
A speedy passage there I gain'd,
　　And wing'd my rapid way.
That moment all the furious throng,
An entrance forcing pour'd along,
　　And fill'd my peaceful cell,*
Where harmless jest and modest mirth,
And cheerful laughter oft had birth,
　　And joy was wont to dwell.
Nor even the Muses' hallow'd fane,
Their lawless fury can restrain,
　　Or check their headlong haste,
They push them from their solemn seat,
Profane their long rever'd retreat,
　　And lay their Pindus waste.
Not yet content—but hoping still
Their impious purpose to fulfil,
　　They force each yielding door;
And whilst their curses load my head,
With piercing steel they probe the bed,
　　And thirst for human gore.
Meanwhile along the sounding shore,
Where Hudson's waves incessant roar,
　　I work my weary way,
And skirt the windings of the tide,
My faithful pupil by my side,
　　Nor wished the approach of day.
At length ascending from the beach,
With hopes revived; by morn I reach
　　The good Palemon's† cot;
Where, free from terror and affright,
I calmly wait the coming night,
　　My weary fear forgot.
'Twas then I scaled the vessel's‡ side,
Where all the amities abide
　　That mortal worth can boast;
Whence with a longing, lingering view,
I bid my much lov'd York adieu,
　　And sought my native coast.
Now all composed, from dangers far,
I hear no more the din of war,
　　Nor shudder at alarms;
But safely sink each night to rest,
No malice rankling through my breast,
　　In freedom's fostering arms.

---

* King's College, now Columbia.
† Mr. Stuyvesant's seat in the Bowery.
‡ Kingfisher, sloop-of-war, bound to England.

Though stripped of most the world admires,
Yet torn by few untamed desires,
   I rest in calm content;
And humbly hope a gracious Lord
Again those blessings will afford,
   Which once his bounty lent.
Yet still for many faithful friends,
Still day by day my vows ascend,
   Thy dwelling, O my God!
Who steady still in virtue's cause,
Despising faction's mimic laws,
   The path of peace have trod.
Nor yet for friend alone—for all
Too prone to heed sedition's call,
   Hear me, indulgent Heaven!
O! may they cast their arms away—
To Thee and George submission pay,
   Repent and be forgiven.

Note D.

In speaking of O'Beirne, allusion was made to some entertaining particulars related of him by Croly. They are recorded in the "Life and Times of Geo. IV." chap. vii., and as the work may not be easily accessible to many of those into whose hands this pamphlet may fall, I give the passage in full:

"Another Irishman, introduced at this period to the Prince, was a memorable instance of the power of accident. This was O'Beirne, afterwards Bishop of Meath, in Ireland. He had been educated at St. Omer's for the Roman Catholic priesthood. Returning to his college from a visit to his friends in Ireland, he happened to stop at the inn of some English village, so humble that its whole stock of provisions was but one shoulder of mutton; which he immediately ordered for dinner. While it was preparing, a post-chaise with two gentlemen stopped to change horses; the roasting shoulder of mutton attracted their appetites; they had travelled some distance, were weary, and they agreed that the next half hour could not be better spent than in dining on what they could get.

"But a new difficulty arose, on their being told that the only dinner in the house belonged to a 'young Irish gentleman above stairs.' The travellers were at first perplexed; but after a little consultation, agreed with the landlady's idea, that the shoulder should be theirs; but that, to save the credit of her house, the young Irishman should be invited to partake of it. She was despatched as ambassadress; but returned, after an ineffectual attempt at persuasion, announcing that 'the young gentleman was not to be softened; but, on the contrary, protested that no two travellers, nor any ten on earth, should deprive him of his dinner.' This menacing message, however, was followed by the appearance of O'Beirne himself, good-humoredly saying, that though he could not relinquish the shoulder of mutton to anybody, yet 'if they would partake of it with him, he would be happy to have their company at dinner.'

"The proposal was pleasantly made and pleasantly accepted. The party sat down; the bottle went round; none of the three was deficient in topics; and before the evening closed, the travellers were so much struck with the appearance and manners of their entertainer, then a very handsome young man, and always a very quick, anecdotical, and intelligent one, that they asked him 'What he meant to do with himself in the world?' His destination for the Irish priesthood was immediately set down as altogether inferior to the prospects which might lie before his abilities in English life. On parting, the travellers gave him their cards, and desired him to call on them on his arrival in London. We may judge of his surprise, when he found that his guests were no less personages than Charles Fox and the Duke of Portland!

"Such an invitation was not likely to be declined. His two distinguished friends kept their promise honorably; and in a short period O'Beirne enjoyed all the advantages of the first society of the empire. What his graceful appearance and manners gained in the first instance was kept by his literary acquirements and the usefulness of his services. He was for a considerable period on a confidential footing in the Duke of Portland's household, and much employed in the party negotiations of the time. Among his lighter labors were two dramas, from the French, which he assisted the Duchess of Devonshire in translating and adapting for the stage; and of whose failure, for they seem to have been blown away by a tornado of criticism, the assistant gallantly bore the blame. But O'Beirne had now securely fastened himself on prosperity, and 'neither domestic treason nor foreign levy,' neither the check of a negotiation nor the overthrow of a drama, could uproot him. On Howe's conciliatory mission to America, O'Beirne was sent with him as chaplain, and in some measure as secretary. The mission was flung into utter scorn by the Americans, as every one predicted that it would be; but the chaplain preached a famous sermon at New York, and brought home the only laurels of the embassy. On Lord Fitzwilliam's fatal appointment to the viceroyalty of Ireland, O'Beirne accompanied him as chaplain and private secretary, and with the usual promise of the first diocese. The viceroyalty lasted but six months; yet six months which were long enough to lay the foundations of the rebellion. The alternate feebleness and violence of this brief government, of whose results the noble viceroy was probably as unconscious as the babe unborn, made the change one of imperious necessity. Yet O'Beirne escaped from the wreck, floated where all was going down around him; and had scarcely reappeared in London, when he was raised to the peerage, and the opulent bishopric of Meath, valued at £8,000 a year. Whether this accession of rank and wealth added equally to his happiness, is a graver question.

"It may well be presumed that they were not gained without envy, nor, at such a time, held without attack. His change of religion, though at an early period of life, and on conviction, was not forgotten by his fellow-students at St. Omer's, who were now scattered through Ireland as priests. His political connections were at an end; their debt had been paid, and except a solitary letter from the Duke of Portland, his English intercourse was closed. The party fiercenesses of Ireland are always bitter in the degree of their unimportance; their patriotism tears the country with the passion and the impotence of children. And to this worthless and nameless strife was a man relegated, who had spent the flower of his days in the first society of England, among women, the 'cynosures' of elegance and fashion; in constant intercourse with men of first-rate ability and national influence; and in the centre and living glare of those great transactions which moved all Europe, and which will shape its history for ages to come.

"The restlessness natural to such a strife, rather than the necessity for reform, urged him to a hasty reform in his diocese. But there is no operation more delicate, under any circumstances; and no reliance on the value of his intentions could shield their practice from long and bitter animadversions. He died a few years ago, after a career which might have made an instructive and curious biography, and no bad manual of 'the art of rising in the world.' "